UPS
and
DOWNS

UPS

and

DOWNS

Memoirs of
Another Time

NIKA HAZELTON

HARPER & ROW, PUBLISHERS, New York
Cambridge, Philadelphia, San Francisco, London
1817 *Mexico City, São Paulo, Singapore, Sydney*

FIRST EDITION

Copyeditor: Inez M. Krech

Designer: Cassandra J. Pappas

Library of Congress Cataloging-in-Publication Data

Hazelton, Nika Standen.
  Ups and downs.

  1. Hazelton, Nika Standen. 2. Cookery writers—
United States—Biography. I. Title.
TX649.H38A3 1989   940.5'2'0924 [B]   88-45515
ISBN 0-06-015742-9

---

89 90 91 92 93 CC/HC 10 9 8 7 6 5 4 3 2 1

*To my grandchildren,
Julian, Melissa, and Amy*

CONTENTS

UPS
and
DOWNS

1. ROME

The nuns used to say, "Be sure to lie straight, legs together, arms crossed on your chest, so that, should you die during the night, you'll meet your Creator with dignity." This was when one of them made the rounds after we had gone to bed in the convent dormitory. Each of us had a little cell, separated from the next by a white curtain that was drawn during the day, but at night when we were in bed the curtains were pulled back. The nun herself slept in a little room at the end of the dormitory, where a night-light burned in front of a large chromo of the Virgin Mary.

The scene is a Sacred Heart convent school in Rome in the early twenties, which I attended both as a day girl and, when my parents were away, as a boarder. We had an agreeable time getting a good deal of liberal education in literature, composition, the arts, history, and geography. Mathematics I never understood, nor was I made to understand it; as for science, it was not considered necessary for girls destined for a comfortable married life, as indeed it was not. One can argue that school should teach you subjects that you would never investigate for yourself. On the other hand, why bother? If one were interested in a specific subject later on, one would find out about it anyway. I remember other things about my convent school: the big white aprons that covered us from neck to ankle, which had to be kept clean for three days—we changed aprons twice a week and had a clean one for Sunday; the broad blue ribbons across our chests that we wore as the Daughters of Mary, with all the medals we had earned for good deeds; the fact that I could say the Rosary faster than anybody and took bets on my speed; the pious ejaculations to which we childishly added naughty endings that rhymed, such as "Sacred Heart of Jesus, I'm so hungry I can't stand it anymore" *(Sacro Cuore del mio Gesù, ho una fame che non ne posso piu);* the glass of red wine we got with our meals, during which we had to be silent while one of the nuns read aloud the life of some favorite saint. The glass of wine was only for the boarders; day girls ate lunch in their own dining room where they also had to be silent and listen to the pious readings of a nun.

When I was a day girl, like all the other day girls I brought my lunch from home in my plain, well-marked lunch box. We all brought with us two eggs or a thin slice of meat, called a *fettina,* and the individual, round fireproof dish called a *tegamino* in which the eggs or meat were cooked, with the blob of butter needed to cook the food. I remember very clearly the small, bent lay sister, the Suora Conversa, who cooked for us day girls. When we came to school in the mornings, we left our lunch boxes near the little gas stove, outside the day girls' dining room, where she fried our eggs or meat. At lunchtime, each day girl would find her lunch box at her assigned seat. The Suora Conversa would rush in with our hot *tegamini,* which she held with a dishrag, anxious to get our food to us as hot as she could manage, since we ate it out of the pan. After we finished eating our bread, cheese, and fruit straight out of our lunch boxes (the convent did not provide any amenities such as plates or napkins), we simply put the dirty *tegamini* back into our boxes. We

2

deposited these where we had left them in the morning, to take home when it was time to go. I used my rather beaten-up, brass-handled *tegamino* for years, eating from it at school and at home.

I remember especially the year in which the nun who taught us art history had piously inked little aprons over the genitals of the statues shown in our art books. But she took us to San Stefano Rotondo, a circular church in which the walls were frescoed with the particularly gruesome and most graphically drawn tortures inflicted on the martyrs of antiquity, pictures where nothing was left to the imagination. When last in Rome a few years ago, I found out, alas, that the church was being renovated and I could not show my husband the scene of my youthful frissons. I also remember the "spiritual bouquets" that we prepared for the visits of eminent prelates to our school. A spiritual bouquet is a listing of prayers said and good deeds done, entered on a pretty card, to be given instead of real flowers to an ecclesiastical dignitary. I can also still do the complicated *broderie anglaise* we were taught, though I never could, and still cannot, understand why one should cut holes in perfectly good cloth just to embroider around them with white thread. Most of all I remember something that I think only possible in the Catholic world of Rome in those times—that in a mixed marriage the sons followed the father's religion and the daughters that of the mother. My father was a Protestant and in order that I should get acquainted with his religion I was sent to the Lutheran pastor's lessons once a week during the school year. I never walked alone in the street. When my mother or a maid could not accompany me to the pastor's house, Mother Superior sent a lay sister to walk with me and wait for me until we both walked back.

I think this last memory describes best the two worlds in which we lived—my mother's Italian one and my father's German-Italian world, which conditioned me from the very beginning to be an onlooker at the various other worlds into which the untidy pile of events, which is my life, plunged me later. At

3

one time or other I have lived in Switzerland, Germany, England, Brazil, and the United States and have been part of these countries, but still I have always essentially remained an observer who refers to the observed as "they." Never in my life have I felt any desire to live where my forebears—even my parents—lived, or to be buried near them in the same cemetery.

This feeling of detachment from my surroundings is also due to the fact that I remember practically nothing of my early childhood and very little of my childhood in general. Of early childhood I have only two memories: falling into a fountain in Villa Borghese in Rome with the feeling of water closing over my face (I do not remember who pulled me out), and the great moment when I was first able to look over our dining room table, set for one of my mother's tea parties. I must have been three or four years old, because our table was high and I was not a particularly tall child.

I remember that the white tablecloth was embroidered to its last inch with *broderie anglaise.* Mercifully, the fashion for *broderie anglaise* has declined in our time. (I do admit that a table spread with such a white, freshly ironed, embroidered linen cloth promoted a feeling of respectable social security very difficult to achieve with our modern, infinitely more practical, but not very classy-looking synthetic cloths.)

Among the many objects crowding my mother's fashionable tea table at ladies' teas were the pearl-handled little serving forks used to spear tiny sandwiches of thinly cut bread spread with butter and anchovy paste, or lemon slices; they were also used for antipasto goodies at formal meals. I still have some of these three-pronged forks, but I must confess I seldom use them because I no longer entertain formally. From my mother's tea table furnishings I still own a very small vertical glass pitcher that held the rum with which some ladies liked to lace their tea; also a very fancy, flowered little china lemon squeezer-pitcher from which freshly squeezed lemon juice could be poured to boost the cups of reviving liquid. Today I use the glass pitcher for flowers, but the squeezer-pitcher stands forlornly in my kitchen cabinet, never used but still kept in memory of a genteel and settled childhood.

I don't seem to remember any feelings of wonder at the world as a child. I took everything as it came and for granted, and missed out on any sensitive revelations of self and world which so many children seem to have; these revelations have always bored me and still bore me as much as ever. I also have never suffered from association of myself with the places where I have lived. The only house I have truly loved was the one where I lived during the most miserable period of my life, when my first marriage was going to hell.

My remaining unencumbered of so much useless baggage of the mind is largely due to my parents. They never spoke of their childhood, and never hearing about it, I was not curious. (For that matter, they seldom spoke of the past, which I regret deeply because their lives had been interesting.) The past was past, as far as I was concerned. A great many years later when my mother, then in her eighties, came to live with me in America, I was very surprised to find out that she did think a lot about certain parts of her life, though, unfortunately, not of the happier ones. But when young, I was never made to confront the past, though this would have been easy in Rome. I was not taught history *in situ,* but rather learned to look at illustrious ruins such as the Forum and Aventine in a visual, ahistorical way—the connections between past and present were never opened to me.

I don't think my parents were interested in children as such. I was their child and I was there, well taken care of and loved, but in no way fussed about because I was a child. I really don't think they knew what to say to a child (and I was an only child), and to this day, I really don't know either. (My grown sons tell me I never treated them as children, and depending on the circumstance and their humor, they are happy or unhappy about this.) I had no duties to perform, no little childhood jobs to do.

All my parents asked of me as a child was to behave in a reasonably civilized manner, and to stay out of their way. They never tried to influence me one way or the other.

From earliest childhood I learned from my parents the value of an orderly household. Well-prepared meals appeared punctually at 1:30 P.M. and 8:30 P.M. on a nicely set family table; clothes were properly washed, ironed, and returned, correctly hung from the shoulders on cloth hangers, to their respective wardrobes. Heels were rushed to the cobbler when run down, and household repairs were taken care of immediately. Our maids, in a time when many Italian maids had to sleep in the kitchen after it had been straightened up after the late Roman dinners, all had their own rooms and regular times off. And there was no question about my getting into their hair or being impertinent to anybody who worked for us. All of this sounds very commonplace and rather depressing as I put it on paper, but the fact remains that all my life I have profited from having lived in an orderly household. Those who have lived with me profited as well, since they, and I, did not have to waste time looking for clothes, preparing last-minute meals to feed screaming children, or falling off wobbly chairs. True, we always had at least one maid, but there were periods when she was not there and when my mother did the chores herself. I am not fond of cleaning house or having to cook day in and day out, but when the alternative was (as it was for so many years) to live in disorder, I myself did what had to be done. And I can only hope that I did my chores without fussing, as they were done in my mother's house. However, my life has not allowed certain refinements of living that I was brought up with. Our stone kitchen floor was scrubbed three times a day, after each meal, which mine has not been, and my husband and sons did not have their shoelaces or their newspapers ironed, as were my father's. However, all my life I have peeled fruit, even grapes, for my father, husband, sons, and assorted friends. I want to stress that there was nothing rigid about our household; the best thing I can say about it was that it just flowed, with only minor ripples. My mother had a rather tempestuous nature, but the easiness of her household must have been rooted in her taking for granted that it was for the woman of the house to make life comfortable for those under her roof, regardless of how she felt about somebody or something. My mother and I have had very great contretemps, but I have always subscribed to this attitude of hers and other women of her age. At this late time of my life one of the few things I can say about myself is that nothing but illness has stopped me from cooking a meal or going to work.

The Jesuits claim that they can mold any child before it reaches the age of five, a belief shared by many liberated souls who scorn—and underestimate—the Jesuits. My own attitude to food was certainly formed at home where food was taken casually, and not as the alpha and omega of life. It went without saying that ingredients should be fresh and carefully cooked; that hot foods must be eaten hot and cold foods consumed cold; and all served in the proper order. The meals were structured in the Italian manner. Breakfast consisted of coffee and milk, fresh bread, butter, and jam, the bread having been delivered early in the morning by the baker's boy.

We ate the main meal of the day at 1:30. The oval dining table was always set with a properly ironed white damask tablecloth and matching napkins. Cloth and napkins carried the same serial number embroidered in cross-stitch with red cotton. (I still have several cloths and napkins to match.) This was done to avoid mixing different patterns of tablecloth and napkins and to ensure equal use of a given cloth and its napkins. Our flatware was big, heavy, and real silver. In addition to a silver salt cellar and matching pepper mill, a bottle of mineral water and two bottles of wine—one white and the other red—stood on the table, each bottle esconced in its silver coaster. (I drank about one finger of wine in a glassful of water.) The food was handed around in serving dishes by one of the maids dressed in a clean white apron.

Usually, our first course consisted of pasta or rice dressed with a simple sauce or *all'inglese,* that is, with only butter and freshly grated Parmesan. In season, a platter of sliced mozza-rella and tomatoes crowned with a scattering of basil leaves and sprinkled with olive oil (known in Rome as *La Caprese,* the Capri female) would come to the table. A great family favorite was baked tomatoes or zucchini stuffed with rice (a Roman specialty) or a plate of slices of rosy prosciutto wrapped around slices of ripe, fragrant cantaloupe. (My mother, several times a week, would accompany a maid on the daily shopping expedition. But my mother, a *signora,* like all the proper *signore* of the time, never carried the smallest parcel herself. When there wasn't anyone to carry her parcels, a *signora* like my mother would arrange to have her purchases sent home.)

The second course was a small, thin slice or two of veal scaloppine or beef *fettine,* quickly sautéed in a little olive oil and wine, and served with a round slice of fresh lemon to zip up the meat. With it came a green vegetable such as spinach, cooked quickly in whatever water clung to it after washing, and then sautéed in olive oil, sometimes with pine nuts and a bit of garlic. If instead of a vegetable a green salad of Boston lettuce accompa-nied the meat, the salad was dressed plainly with oil and small amounts of vinegar, salt, and pepper. Here I should say that we only used the finest cold-pressed, nonacid olive oil from our relatives' country estates. To this day I say "pfui" to the horrid concoctions sold as salad dressings in this country.

Since one starch at a meal was considered sufficient, we never ate potatoes with our meat when the first course consisted of pasta or rice. We finished the meal with a bite of cheese, such as Bel Paese or old Parmesan, followed by fresh fruit. With the fruit came individual chased-brass finger bowls, in which a slice of fresh lemon floated on the water. We washed our grapes in the finger bowls before rinsing our fingers in the water and indulging in a discreet wiping of our mouths with the wet corner of our napkins. The cheese course was consumed with proper cheese knives and cheese forks, and fruit followed on separate plates, to be peeled with the silver fruit knives that I still use at my own table.

Filoni, long loaves of Italian bread, freshly baked, were fetched by a maid for dinner and supper. As with all our Italian friends and relatives, a meal without bread was inconceivable. But butter never came to the table with the bread unless my father asked for it specifically at suppertime to go with the cold cuts he liked to eat. Dinner ended with little demitasse cups of espresso, served always in the little salon with the green damask-covered chairs.

In the afternoon, my mother might have a tea party or be going to one and I, if hungry, had a handful of the dry cookies Italians excel at. I love and eat them to this day, but my husband has always claimed that they come from a Dead Sea bakery, where all Italian-style cookies are baked.

Supper, at half past eight, was a simple meal made up of leftovers from lunch such as pasta fried in an omelette, a *frittata,* cold cuts or scrambled eggs with home-fried potatoes, and a salad. As all Italians did and still do, we ate our eggs at supper and not at breakfast.

Much later in life, I found out that my mother had written the finest German-language cookbook on Italian food, which, I don't know why, had an Italian title: *Cosi si Mangia in Italia.* Whether the book sold well and where it was sold, I have never discovered because my mother did not talk about it, even when I wrote cookbooks myself to make a living. But, who knows, maybe I inherited my interest in food from my mother, along with some other character traits. Ah, well.

My parents entertained frequently with varying degrees of splendor. Friends just took potluck with us and drank our home wine. Acquaintances to be honored in a just, but moderate, measure got bottled wines like Chianti and Soave, which in the old days were not as commercialized as they are now. For really fancy dinner parties, when my mother summoned waiters with white gloves, my father served his specially imported Burgundy and hock, as well as Upmen cigars, which came straight from Cuba. On those special occasions I did not take my meal with my betters, but all dressed up, combed and shiny, was allowed to come in with the coffee to be kissed, fussed about, and sent back to my room.

My father was German and my mother Italian. But it was she who was courageous, hardworking, authoritarian, and, on the whole, pessimistic and inflexible, whereas he was jolly, fun-loving, easygoing, fair, and beloved by all who met him. *È tanto simpatico,* the Italians used to say of Otto, whom I called by his first name, whereas my mother was invariably Mama to me. My father belonged to that group of Germans who were very cultured and artistic and as much a part of Rome as the Romans. The *Deutsches Rom* tradition goes back to a time even before Goethe in classical Germany, and it formed a bond between Germans and Italians that only Hitler managed to tear apart. Interestingly, the majority of the Germans living in Rome never learned to speak Italian properly. In German they conversed fluently and learnedly on the topics close to their minds—art, philosophy, literature; but in Italian they spoke the most ordinary, colloquial language, though they read widely on their favorite subjects in Italian. My father was among them. Although he had lived in Italy for decades and wanted to live nowhere else, his language remained German. The three of us spoke German at home, but I spoke Italian with my mother. I learned French as a little girl at the Sacré Coeur School and English when I was about eight years old. My first English teacher was an old English miss, a determinedly cheerful old spinster and as British as they come, who had spent her life in Rome teaching English. My mother frequently invited her for lunch because the poor woman was said to be so hard up that she could afford only tea and a bun for meals. Needless to say, it was taken for granted that one should know languages if one were a woman—French was expected, and English was desirable even then, before it had become the kind of *lingua franca* it is now throughout the world.

Everybody has his or her own Rome, and ours was that of the Germans and the Romans. My father's Rome and his Italy too, as I know from the notebooks he kept on his travels, were classical. Reading Goethe's *Italian Journey,* I now realize how strongly my father was influenced by Goethe and the classical Italy of Greece and Rome. When my father had first come to Italy from Germany, just before the turn of the century, he had been a very young man, a socialist whose speeches had offended the kaiser, so that in order to avoid imprisonment he had had to leave Berlin. There he had been a part of the avant-garde circle of writers and socialists such as Arno Holz and Ebert, who later became Germany's first republican president. The socialists with whom my father remained friendly came into power in Germany after the First World War when the Weimar Republic began, all of which affected my father's career, which I will go into later.

How it came about I do not know (and how I regret never having asked him, my mother, or others who knew my father at that time), but my father started a publishing house in Rome around the turn of the century. It published art books on classical Rome, the Sistine Chapel, the Campagna Romana, and so forth, in German. I still have some of these books, which are lavishly illustrated with photographs, intellectual in their approach and execution, well printed on paper still pristinely white, and beautifully bound in linen. They are still useful historical guides; the ones I constantly use are two small pocket dictionaries—one an encyclopedia of saints and their symbols, and the other a who's who of mythological figures.

From what I have been able to piece together, in those days my father and his friends led a carefree, jolly life in Rome, a *vie de bohème* life, making merry in their favorite trattoria over immense quantities of wine from the Roman hills. All were artists and writers, drinking in the liberated air of Rome after the stifling Germany of the kaiser. They did not mingle with the German embassy people or the learned professors who were excavating or studying the Rome of the past. When they married Roman girls, which they frequently did, the girls came not from the aristocracy or from the bourgeoisie, but from the common people of Rome, and often they were artists' models. Many of the artists became famous in Germany, notably the etchers Klinger and Greiner. They belonged to that before-World-War-I avant-garde of artists and writers that did so much to sweep away the stuffiness of the Kaiser Wilhelm era, all antimacassars and plush and hidden homosexuality, coupled with court prayers and an empress whose sole ideas were the three K's: *Kinder, Küche, Kirche*—children, kitchen, and church. As my father used to say, Wagner would never have been able to have his Ring produced in Berlin if the court, and especially the empress, had realized what was going on in the trilogy, from Wotan cheating his workmen in *Das Rheingold* to Siegfried carrying on with his sister and his Aunt Brunhilde later on. But, my father said, it was all sung in alliterative verse, and that saved the show.

My father loved books and had thousands of them—each one with his own bookmark designed by Otto Greiner. His famous library included all of Goethe's works and almost everything written about Goethe in German and Italian. Like Goethe, he adored the antique, Greek or mostly Roman, and was indifferent to the Middle Ages and the Renaissance. His enormous library was destroyed by the Allied bombings of Milan, along with almost all our other possessions.

As I am writing this, I hear the interpreters of writers' psyches say, "Ah, she was stuck on her father, and why does she not write about her mother?" I was stuck on my father for sure, sharing his love of books, his politics, and his intellectual preoccupations. But my mother's influence was equally strong. The reason that I will come to her later is that the Rome I knew as a child was still the Rome of my classicist father.

When I was a child in Rome some sixty years ago, there was still a great deal of its nineteenth-century past to be seen. True, we had telephones and electric lights and electric irons. But though our ice came in hunks to be stored in the brown wooden icebox (a bowl underneath the hole in the bottom caught the water from the melting ice), we could—and did—take ourselves to the Appian Way for walks and the picking of cyclamens without seeing another person for miles. Our usual transportation was either the tramway or the horse-drawn cab, the Botticella, whose rather tired horses wore straw hats against the summer sun with an air of raffish abandon. On special occasions, such as New Year's Day and Easter Sunday, my father used to rent a car for a more distant classical destination, such as Ostia Antica. As I said, my father was fond of moseying around classical ruins. The Campagna Romana, the countryside around Rome, was still full of noble Roman fragments of aqueducts and the like, but empty of people. In the winter it was the grazing site of the sheep of the Sardinian shepherds (at least they were known as Sardinian), who looked straight out of eighteenth-century engravings with their wide brown hats, large cloaks thrown carelessly over one shoulder, and their white leggings crisscrossed by the strings of their sandals. They used to play the bagpipes in a naïve but very plaintive way when they came to town selling their reed baskets of exquisite snowy ricotta cheese. (Turned out on a plate, the ricotta showed the basket's erratic shape and pattern.) The *pifferari,* as the Romans called these Sardinian shepherd bagpipe players, were especially visible around Christmas and the New Year and at Epiphany, when they played at the great toy market of Piazza Navona. In those days the Christmas tree had not found its place in a Roman home, nor had Santa Claus; the *befana,* a benevolent witch with a headscarf, brought presents to Italian children. The Romans treated the *befana* market in the big Piazza Navona like a village fair, thronging the stalls filled with candy, factory-made simpering cloth dolls, simple handmade cars, and other wooden toys; we had not yet entered the age of plastics. (Many years later a Roman friend showed me the toys her grandparents had bought over the years in the Piazza Navona *befana* market; they were utterly charming examples of village art.) January is a dark month in Rome, and I think I remember the contrast between the hissing acetylene lamps that illuminated the stalls with violence, and the Piazza Navona white marble fountains shrouded in misty darkness.

As a child, and as long as my parents had their own household which I still call home, we celebrated Christmas the German way. This meant that the presents we exchanged were brought by the *Christkind,* the Holy Babe, on the evening of December 24, also the time when the Christmas tree candles were lit for the first time. Since Christmas Eve was the *real* Christmas to all Germanic people, like them, we always celebrated it strictly *en famille.* Christmas Day, called *der erste Feiertag* (the first festival) in German, was not very interesting to a child who had already received her presents. It was reserved for the festive meal in the middle of the day, and for visiting and receiving visits from friends and relatives. Since my parents did not like to go out on Christmas Day, people streamed in and out of the house all afternoon and evening. But mercifully, apart from having to wish a Happy Christmas to all comers, I was left alone with my presents.

Every year, early in December, my father felt nostalgic for the Christmases of his own childhood, so much so that he wanted to re-create them as well as he could. My mother, a nonsentimental Roman *signora,* deferred to his wishes because she was a dutiful wife and also because she enjoyed any doings that would make her shine as a homemaker. Together, my parents succeeded in making Christmas into the most wonderful event of the year, and making me, their only child, wish to celebrate Christmas as I did when I was a child, wherever I was, and as well as I could.

On the first of the four Advent Sundays that precede Christmas, my mother lit the first of the four white candles (one for each Sunday) of the *Advents-kranz,* a traditional pine wreath she had put in the middle of the dining-room table, where it served as a centerpiece throughout the Christmas season. I was given my glittering Advent calendar, which, beginning on December 1, marked the twenty-four days before Christmas. Each day, I punched open one of the calendar's little numbered windows, which showed a winter scene and plain pine trees, until the last and by far the biggest window revealed a gorgeous, candlelit Christmas tree. On the same Sunday evening my mother, complaining *sotto voce* about the inconvenience of Christmas, locked the door to the *salottino,* the little salon next to the dining room. The reason for this, my mother said, was to give the *Christkind* a chance to rest between his labors of making Christmas for good children.

Early in December, I had also written or dictated my letter to the *Christkind,* stating my wishes for my Christmas presents. (My mother told me that I always wanted books, even before I was able to read, as well as building blocks, preferably blocks in the shape of columns, arches, and pediments.) I put the letter under my pillow at bedtime, and when it was gone in the morning, I knew that the *Christkind* had taken it while I slept. I have often tried to remember when I stopped believing in the gift-bringing Holy Babe. Since for the life of me I cannot remember, the transition from believer to nonbeliever must have been a totally painless one.

Early in December, too, my mother and the maids started baking what seemed to me an infinity of cookies. I was allowed into the usually sternly *verboten* kitchen to lick the cookie pans before they were washed. (Licking clean cake, cookie, or dessert pots or pans before they were washed used to be the children's prerogative in many German households.) The cookies were baked according to their ripening and keeping properties; the most fragile and delicate among them were made only during the last two pre-Christmas days. Honey cookies and peppernuts were baked first, because they had to "ripen" for several weeks. Since my father wanted to nosh on all his favorites, my mother produced scores of Cinnamon Stars, Vanilla Pretzels, Chocolate Loaves, jam-filled Linzers, flat Mazurkas, Hazelnut Rings, Almond Macaroons, and pale, anise-flavored Springerle. My mother concentrated especially on the cookies my father loved best of all: whitish, buttery, crisp morsels shaped like a capital letter S. The cookies were cut out with our old-fashioned cutters in the shape of squares and diamonds, and in the old Christmas shapes of Holy Babes, oxen, asses, camels, and birds; these cutters we had inherited from my father's grandmother. Every single cookie was frosted with gaily colored confectioners' sugar and sprinkled with little silver balls or with the rainbow-colored sprinklers that are known as "hundreds and thousands." The finished cookies were stored in layers divided by clean white papers in the big square tins of my mother's beloved bittersweet Amaretti cookies, saved for many years for just this purpose.

The week before Christmas, my mother decorated the apartment in the German manner she had learned from my father. She wedged pine boughs behind mirrors and pictures, and she filled every vase in the house with pine greens. We never hung a wreath on the outside of the apartment's front door, as people do in the United States, but when you came in, the look of the place as well as the sweet rosiny scent of the pine needles told you at once that this was Christmastime. With increasing frequency, especially near the locked *salottino*, I would find bits of pine and strands of silvery tinsel left behind by the *Christkind* resting in the Christmas room, so my parents said.

Finally it was Christmas Eve, and the maids were shining the last piece of silverware after an incredibly thorough housecleaning. In the morning, the big square cookie tins filled with their goodies came out of their hiding places, which my cookie-hungry father could never find. In the dining room my mother, after having made sure that my father was out of the house, filled a number of large, scallop-edged paper plates with assorted cookies. These *bunte Teller* (multicolored plates) were red, with a particularly resplendently decorated and candlelit Christmas tree on the bottom. (*Bunte Teller*, true to German custom, were given to all who came to the house during the Christmas week, in addition to their usual presents and tips.) I can still see the *bunte Teller*, all filled and lined up on our dining room mahogany sideboard, which for the occasion had been cleared of all silver objects that showed we were a respectable family. After lunch, memorable because for once I did not have to eat up all the food on my plate, I was given a bath and dressed in my best clothes. Then my father took me to a carol service in Rome's Lutheran church, where we all sang in German the old songs of the German Middle Ages, of Mary rocking her babe and of the Rose that sprang from Jesse's tree. We came home in the dusk of a late December afternoon. The apartment appeared to be deserted and my father disappeared after having told me to wait for the *Christkind* in the dark dining room. How well I remember my sitting and waiting, my heart in my mouth and so excited as to be reduced to stillness. Finally, I heard the sound of the Christmas silver bell and the large door between the dining room and the *salottino* burst open. There stood the big Christmas tree, shining in all its glory of gold and silver glass balls, with all its candles lit to a single, immense light. Then I knew that Christmas had really come at last.

My parents and the maids, all decked out in their Sunday best, were waiting for me. We all admired the Christmas tree and embraced, wishing each other a Merry Christmas. Then, as always, my father, by the light of the tree's candles and with a catch in his voice, read in German the story of the Nativity, according to the Gospel of Saint Luke. I must admit that I was not listening carefully; instead, I looked at the big silver tinsel star that topped the tree and symbolized the Star of Bethlehem, which was always the first ornament to go on the Christmas tree and the last to come down when the tree was dismantled. I greeted the familiar crèche and its old Neapolitan painted wooden figures that nestled on the white tablecloth draped over the foot of the big, sturdy pine tree. Finally, after casting longing glances at my pile of presents on a nearby table, I was told by my parents to go and see what the *Christkind* had brought me.

According to the old German custom, our presents were never wrapped in gift paper. Here and there in the room, each person's gifts were stacked up in individual piles. In our family, Christmas presents never included practical things like warm underwear, stockings, or gloves, but only heart's desire of rather unnecessary things. Since I did not like dolls, but always wanted books to read or to be read from or to look at, I invariably received books, as well as coloring pencils, paint boxes, building blocks, and the like. My father also received books, and for my mother there were fancy gloves, handbags, and perfume. One thrilling Christmas, my mother found a Persian lamb fur coat among her presents. The maids were given a large cash tip, made less utilitarian by some fancy soap and other toiletries. And everybody also received one of my mother's *bunte Teller*.

As for my own presents for my parents, all I remember is that they consisted of simple things made by myself. There were pictures in crayon, little mats woven from strands of colored paper, braided strands of wool. When I learned to write, there were thank-you letters on writing paper prettied up with my own designs. In those days, children always made their own presents for the grown-ups; shopping for presents by a child was as unheard of as a trip to the moon. Furthermore, children had no money of their own, and grown-ups never thought of giving them any, whatever the purpose.

How is it that after a lifetime I remember the Christmases of my childhood in such detail? Whatever the reason, I do, and I think my memory is set by the sameness of the holiday ritual, year after year.

For Christmas Eve supper we always had a meal of my father's simple favorites of scrambled eggs with home-fried potatoes, pickled beets, and pumpernickel with Swiss cheese. One year I was struck when butter appeared on the table. My mother, however, hastened to tell me that the butter was only for my father, who, she said despairingly, liked to butter his bread when he ate cheese. (As in every Italian household, plain bread was served at every meal, cut up into slices and served in a napkin-lined round little basket.) Thinking back, I assume that my mother went against her own customs to cater to him, since the bread was not the usual long, crisp Italian loaf of everyday eating, but dark pumpernickel bread that had to be bought in a specialty store.

As far as I was concerned, nothing of interest happened on Christmas Day. I played with my new presents and ate as many cookies as I pleased from my own *bunter Teller.* My parents were relaxed, enjoying the afternoon visits from their friends, and the Christmas tree released a sweet scent of pine needles and candle wax throughout the house. We ate our big dinner in the middle of the day. The maids had a free evening to canoodle with their sweethearts. Every year, when the maids had gone off, my mother used to remark that she only hoped the girls would not get pregnant and have to be sent back home to their villages.

Since Christmas was my father's prerogative, our meal was a German one. We started with a powerful concentrated beef bouillon served in cups and accompanied by cheese sticks, and went on to a substantial main course of herbed veal served with roast potatoes and two vegetables, and finished with meringue with lots of whipped cream. First course and dessert remained the same year after year, but the main course could be roast goose, which was served with applesauce. My mother did not care for goose, either to eat or to cook, but as I said before, Christmas was for my father.

Having described how things were a long time ago, and in another country as well, I want to express myself on my present-day Christmas. What it comes down to is that I believe in painless Christmases in these days of no or little holiday help. This means a meal that can be prepared beforehand any old time, and then frozen and reheated when needed. Thus I have gone in for chili, an agreeable change from all that sweetness of holiday fare. As to the chili that follows, all of my guests have said it is the best chili they ever ate. I can only hope that my readers will at least make the chili once to see if they agree. Bob Holleron, an extremely good-looking gentleman and a great cook as well, gave me the recipe many years ago in San Antonio, Texas, a city that I love.

Preface: Essentially, *chile con carne,* truly a Tex-Mex dish, is nothing more than a well-designed stew. As in other stews, certain rules are important. First, every bit of fat, which would make the chili greasy, must be trimmed off the meat. This means that if you want to come up with six pounds of trimmed meat, you must buy eight pounds. Second, the meat must be thoroughly browned. This takes quite a bit of time, since the meat at first gives off a lot of water, which must evaporate before the meat can brown. Third, the meat is best browned in a good vegetable oil. (The traditional fat in which to brown chili meat is lard, which is all right if you like the flavor.) When a large quantity of chili is made, it is best to brown the meat in batches. Fourth, make sure that the spices are very fresh, or the chili won't have any flavor. Fifth, don't put any beans in the chili; they are strictly a side dish.

BOB HOLLERON'S CHILE CON CARNE

6 pounds (trimmed weight) lean boneless beef, such as round, sirloin, or lean chuck (buy 8 pounds)

½ to ¾ cup salad oil

1 large onion, cut into tiny dice

1 large garlic clove, crushed

8 ounces canned tomato sauce

2 cups hot water

6 tablespoons first-class chili powder

4 tablespoons ground cuminseed

1 tablespoon cracked black pepper

1 tablespoon salt

½ tablespoon paprika
generous dash of Tabasco

3 tablespoons masa harina (available in Latin groceries) or flour

6 tablespoons warm water

Cut the beef, which must be absolutely free of all fat, into ¼- to ½-inch dice. (It is important not to use *ground* meat since it does not make a flavorful chili.) Heat ¼ cup of the salad oil in a large, heavy frying pan. Add a batch of meat, not crowding the pan. Cook over moderate heat, stirring almost constantly, until the meat is nicely brown and there is no liquid in the frying pan. (This takes longer than one expects—at least five minutes.) As each batch is finished browning, transfer it to a heavy casserole large enough to take all the meat. Repeat the process, adding oil as needed, until all the meat is browned. Cook the onion and the garlic in the frying pan until the onion is soft but not brown. Add the tomato sauce, water, chili powder, cuminseed, pepper, salt, paprika, and Tabasco. Blend thoroughly and stir the mixture into the browned meat in the casserole. Cover the casserole. Simmer over low heat, stirring frequently, for one or two hours. Add a little hot water if at any point there is danger of scorching. If the chili is thinner than desired (different cuts of meat throw off different amounts of water), blend the *masa harina* and the 6 tablespoons of water into a smooth paste. Stir into the chili and cook uncovered, stirring frequently, until thickened. Serves 12 to 15.

Notes: 1. If the meat was properly trimmed and lean to begin with, there should be no fat in the chili. However, if there is some, skim it off with paper towels or refrigerate the chili and then remove the fat that has risen to the surface. 2. For a hotter chili, use more chili powder and more Tabasco. The above listed proportions, however, have proved to be successful. 3. Serve the chili with *frijoles* and *salsa,* and plenty of beer; do not waste wine on chili.

By New Year's Eve, the tree had been lit so many times during Christmas week that the first set of Christmas tree candles had to be replaced with new, equally bright-colored ones. At the stroke of midnight, I was allowed to wish my parents a Happy New Year, because, as a special privilege, I had been allowed to stay up. Since we invariably stayed home on New Year's Eve, celebrating it with a few friends, my parents liked to indulge in the old German game of guessing the future with *Bleigiessen.* This consisted of melting small bits of lead (where it came from, I never found out, since I would not have dreamt of asking my parents) in a spoon over a candle flame, and then plunging the molten lead into a nearby basin of cold water. The hot metal, in contact with the cold water, disintegrated into a multitude of twisted shapes, which were interpreted as a portent of things to come. I can remember melting my own lead, but I cannot recall what I thought of the little untidy heaps of gray metal.

On January 6, Epiphany, my mother took the Christmas tree down. The pine was shedding its needles, and, anyway, it was no longer the wonderful novelty of Christmas Eve. The candles, or their remains, were pried loose from the holders and thrown away, and all the glass ornaments and the crèche went to sleep in their boxes for another year. As the last thing, the maids freed the tree from its holder and dragged it out to the service door. All of this happened so quickly and so without any fuss that I paid little attention to the funeral of that year's Christmas.

Christmas was also the time when children recited poems in praise of the Nativity in the Aracoeli church on Rome's Capitol. Who the children were or why they were chosen I do not know. But I remember being taken into the crowded, gloomily lit church after my mother literally dragged me up the long flight of stairs that leads to the Capitol; the church is on the left side as you mount from Piazza Venezia. I cannot remember what the festively dressed little boys and girls recited, but I was extremely impressed with their courage in standing before such a crowd. I think I must have seen the last of these traditional Roman Christmas events. (No, I don't know when it started, nor when it stopped.) Apart from their famous crèche, Santa Maria in Aracoeli also housed a miraculous statue of *Gesù Bambino,* the Infant Christ. On request, one or the other of the friars of Santa Maria used to take the Bambino to the sick and dying to help them in their agonies. Whenever the city of Rome was in distress or threatened by the plague, so I read in an early nineteenth-century chronicle, the Bambino was paraded in great pomp throughout Rome's streets. Some years ago when in Rome, I went up to Aracoeli to look properly at the church. Seeing one of the friars I asked him if the Bambino would still travel to a sick person's house as he did in my childhood. "Very seldom," the friar said, "and only to people with serious intentions who are known to the Church." The poor Bambino had to be smuggled out under protective cover or the authorities would arrest him, the friar added.

As a child I also saw the last of another Roman tradition, the *Carnevale dei Bambini,* the Children's Carnival. Rome's carnival in the eighteenth century was almost as famous as that of Venice, but I believe that the Children's Carnival was a Roman custom. I still remember seeing little boys and girls strolling on the Via Nazionale and other major Roman streets dressed as Columbia and Pulcinella, Louis XV, or the Fairy Queen; they were on their way to the *Ballo dei Bambini,* the Children's Ball. I was told by my mother, who disapproved of such things, that the children were simply showing off or being shown off by their beaming, fat *popolani* parents, common people, as she shook off the confetti and streamers which the children threw at one and all.

Another vague memory is that of the famous Roman wet nurses, the *balie Romane,* peasant women from the Sabine or other Roman mountain villages, who suckled the infants of well-to-do Romans. These Junoesque figures, all bosom, flashing eyes, and raven hair, used to congregate with their charges in the Pincio Garden. There I used to be taken by my mother or one of the maids to roll my hoop as we walked along leafy alleys, lured by their shade, and such a relief from the Roman sun. (Our walks invariably included an hour or so spent in front of the little ramshackle stand of *Il Teatro dei Pupazzi.* The puppet theater kept us all spellbound with its villainous villains and demure maidens defended by intrepid brothers and fathers.) The *balie* were dressed in the ritual costume of a white blouse worn under a black corselet and a full red skirt. The pride of each *balia* was her jewelry of gold and red coral, the more and the bigger, the better her necklaces and earrings. The jewelry was provided by the employers of these ultra *saftig* women, who considered owning jewelry a point of honor. Since the employers were as likely to produce children as frequently as the wet nurses and to have their various young suckled by the same woman, a clever *balia* armed with the native shrewdness of her peasant environment could and did accumulate quite a lot of jewelry in her turns of duty. (*"Un bacio al pupo e un pizzico alla balia,"* a kiss for the kid and a pinch for the wet nurse, used to be a common Roman way of leave-taking.)

What other visual memories of a Rome that is no longer? I still see the strong young men dressed from hat to toe in bright red soutanes whom the Romans called *gamberi cotti,* boiled lobsters. They were seminarians from the Collegium Germanicum, and they were not the only apprentice priests to brighten the dark streets of old Rome. The seminarians of the different nations who studied in Rome were clothed in different colors; I think the Scottish appeared in light violet soutanes. But it was the flashing red of the Germans that stole the show.

Another sight of the time when tourists in Rome were still called foreigners was the market of the Piazza Montanara. There the traffic was largely in servant girls and laborers from the mountain villages of the countryside around Rome and the Abruzzi. The bewildered rustics had come to Rome to find work, and Piazza Montanara was the place a boss or a *signora* went to find a working man or a maid. A puppet theater enchanted those poor illiterates and a barely literate public scribe wrote letters for them with a goose quill pen from early morning into the night. I don't know if my mother ever found a servant girl on the Piazza Montanara, but she always said that those barefoot children of nature knew nothing but how to make very good fettuccine. They had learned the art of pasta-making from early youth since the families were too poor to afford store-bought pasta. Invariably, the pasta was fettuccine; the flour usually came from a patch of home-grown wheat. When eggs were used for the fettuccine (which were incorrectly made more often than not with flour and water only), the eggs came from the inevitable chickens that belonged to each household and furnished the meat that was strictly holiday fare among the very poor rural populations of the Italy of that time. In spite of the miserable pay, these poor country girls wanted to work in Rome, because at least they would be able to eat a couple of meals each day, and be in the great city—understandably enough of an advantage when one knew their home surroundings.

Everybody has his or her Rome, depending on the personal traditions, preferences, or expectations. The city offers something for every mood, and in contrast to the restrictions of Florence, Rome is ample, rich in dark greenery and open spaces to set off or to contrast the layer cake of civilizations that this city is. Also, again compared with Florence, Rome is much more damaged by modern development in the form of jerry-built apartment houses and cars by the hundreds of thousands occupying every inch of available public space. The traffic is unspeakable; I am convinced that every Roman owns two cars; one for driving around and the other for parking in perpetuity, as a status symbol, no doubt, thus making doubly sure that Rome is an utterly impossible town to move around in, on foot or on wheels.

Equally appalling are the cheaply built large concrete apartment houses that are disfiguring any Italian city's outskirts. As poor as the leafy little old huts you still see occasionally in outer Rome's streets may be, they are still of a human scale, unlike the new concrete tenements, put there without adequate water or sewage, stark naked in the yellow dust, and without the simplest landscaping. Only the plants in the windows and on the rickety little balconies allow the inhabitants to show the great basic of the Italian character, the love for growing plants and flowers. "Forget about transportation," said the Italian priest who took me around, commenting on the good nature of the people who had to live there.

I was born in a very historic *palazzo;* the owner, a prince, rented out the lesser apartments to people like us. Dividing the noble building into apartments and renting them out is still the standard way of making some money from the inherited noble pile; the owners retain whatever apartment they can afford as well as the use of the *saloni* of the *piano nobile.* This "noble" floor, usually all antique, fragile damask furniture, ancestral portraits, and old paintings under immensely high ceilings, lies on the first floor, counting floors Italian style, or on the second floor, as we count floors in America.

My father loved living in Rome's historic past, *la vecchia Roma,* which allowed him to combine his interests in classical or romantic Rome with my well-being, such as taking me for walks on the Forum Romanum. There, my father brooded on a broken piece of antique masonry while I looked for violets and cyclamens in what was then still an abandoned semi-jungle of ruins where a few earnest Germans and Englishmen walked about, guidebook in hand. My mother, however, did not like living in dark, old downtown Rome. Thus we moved uptown into a modern apartment house on a wide, tree-lined avenue between Porta Pinciana and Porta Veneta. The apartment was a standard, spacious bourgeois model, and it consisted of two bedrooms, a dining room, two *salotti* (drawing rooms), one-and-a-half bathrooms, and another room off the kitchen where the maids slept. In the winter, we had central heating, for which we paid extra. The apartment was expensive, my mother complained, but, as she admitted, worth it. In our old apartment, which, unlike many old apartments, boasted radiators in every room, the heat was produced by a hot air furnace in the kitchen. The furnace ate coal like mad, so that my mother constantly had to remind the maids to bring up more coal from our little cellar in the *palazzo*'s basement. In our new apartment we still had the necessity of producing our own hot water via a boiler, which sat in the bathroom over the tub. When we moved uptown, my mother had treated herself to a gleaming white new boiler, with a pilot light so that one did not need to light it whenever hot water was needed. All one had to do was open the hot water taps in the bathroom or in the kitchen, and after a minute or two, piping hot water would gush out. (My mother, who spent the last decade of her life with us in New York and never liked this country, could never get over the fact that in the United States winter heat and unlimited hot water were always included in the rent.) Loath to throw out the copper boiler she had replaced in her move, my mother first called an artisan to dismantle the boiler and save the valuable copper parts. Then she turned the copper over to another artisan who fashioned a gigantic salad bowl from it. A third artisan then engraved the copper bowl with baroque swirls and leaves down to the last inch of its surface and lid. The fourth artisan then silver plated this splendid object. I still have the bowl, and whenever I have served salad in it, it has always been admired as a very fine thing. But even more than the bowl, I have admired my mother's ingenuity.

In the new apartment, my father's library was housed in the larger of the two *salotti,* which also held my father's own very cherished possession: a large, square radio, which at that time, around the early twenties, was still a novelty. He listened to it a great deal while reading. My mother's piano lived in the smaller *salotto,* a formal room into which I was not allowed by myself; I think it was furnished with green damask-covered Louis XV chairs, suitable for *signora di buona famiglia,* a lady of a good family, as my mother considered herself.

Over the piano hung an impressionistic oil portrait of Madame H., a close friend of my mother's and the wife of an attaché at the French legation. Her husband had divorced her shortly after the portrait had been painted; their story could have been written by de Maupassant. It seems that Monsieur H., undressing his wife one evening, noticed that her corsets were laced up in a manner different from that of Madame's maid. From this he deduced that somebody other than the maid had laced Madame's corsets, ergo, that Madame had been unfaithful and that her lover had laced her stays. Confronted with this, Madame broke down, confessed, and became divorced. What happened to her eventually, I don't know. Mama kept the portrait, however. Another friend of my mother's, a dumpy and dowdy old Frenchwoman, was known to us as *la veille d'un crime* or "the eve of a crime." "I am *à la veille d'un crime,*" the lady cried out passionately whenever she came to the house, meaning that she was about to kill her son-in-law, a Persian who lived in Teheran with Madame's daughter, his wife. As far as I know, the crime was never committed because the couple never came to Rome and *la veille d'un crime* never left Rome. But she did play four hands on the piano with my mother, largely Beethoven symphonies and Verdi operas. My mother played a great deal of standard classical repertoire; she never played anything composed later than Schubert. I shall never cease to be thankful to her for familiarizing me from earliest childhood with Haydn, Mozart, Schubert, and Beethoven.

I have often wondered how a person's appearance and character can belie each another. My mother was a classical Roman beauty, antique noble-matron style, but a rather bourgeois soul was covered by her aristocratic appearance. (The contrary was true of my father.) Her youth had been very difficult and financially unstable. My mother hardly ever spoke of her family, so that I cannot tell much about them, interesting as they must have been. I never knew my grandparents, but my grandfather, Giacomo Leoni, from Bergamo in northern Italy, was some sort of a descendant of Giacomo Leoni, the Italian architect who rose to success in Palladian England. My grandfather liked to have a room in his Roman flat for the exclusive use of his birds (canaries, I believe), where they flew about—no cages for them. When one bird escaped into the rest of the house, the family had to get it back quickly, or hell would break loose. My maternal grandfather's temper was quick, and he looked it, judging from his oil portrait—flashing black eyes, fierce brows, a big, very black beard in the familiar patriarchal Victorian manner—that also hung in the *salotto*. My grandfather was not a natural provider. Most of the time life was from hand to mouth, though he must have had good jobs; for instance, he was involved in the building of the opera house in São Paulo, Brazil, as I found out quite by chance from a local Brazilian brochure on the subject when I was in Brazil in the thirties. He also built for the Turkish sultans in Istanbul and in Asia Minor, where my mother was born in 1874, in a town then called Izmid.

It appears that my grandfather, in order to keep his five children amused as they traveled on muleback in Asia Minor (what for, I don't know), imported an Italian hand organ which headed the little caravan; whether he also imported an organ grinder, I don't know. The memories of my mother's Turkish past reached well into my own childhood in the shape of very large pieces of curlicued bronze banisters and some enormous bolts of beige woven cotton fabric. The banisters were the superfluous parts of the banisters of a palace in Constantinople which my grandfather built and which, allegedly, later became the Russian Embassy there, my mother once murmured to me. They invariably hung on the walls of the entrance to the apartment. I am happy to say that these bronze enormities must have been left behind when, very much later, my parents moved to Milan. A bolt of dun-colored cotton fabric was another relic of those long-ago days. Each summer, throughout my early childhood, the fabric was made into summer dresses for me. I hated the "Turkish dresses," but my mother thought them practical and quite good-looking. But I did like the sailor suits I wore summer and winter. The winter ones were made of navy blue serge and the summer ones of a light blue cotton. On Sundays, however, my suits were made of a heavy white twill in winter and a closely woven white cotton in summer. These sailor suits were very fashionable in my childhood, and were liked by grown-ups for their neatness. They consisted of two parts: over a skirt with an elastic waistband went a middy blouse, with a large square collar that sported navy or white piping around the edges; in front it was tied with a black silk tie. The matching hat was a round white sailor's cap; around it was a blue ribbon that ended in two loose bits. How well I remember how the two ribbon ends hit my cheeks when I ran! To my sorrow, and also to the sorrow of every child I knew, there was no ship's name spelled out in large gold letters on the front part of the ribbon. And to my shame, so that I should not lose the cap, an elastic tied to both its sides held the cap in place by going under my chin.

My grandfather had been married before, and Zio Beppo, a mild old man living on his meager professor's pension when I knew him, was his oldest son. I have no idea who Beppo's mother was, but my mother's mother was something else. Her mother, my great grandmother, Mina Rauh, was born (this is all I know of her) somewhere near Stuttgart in Germany and married a rich landowner who died when she was twenty-six years old. (Her charming Winterhalter-like portrait still hangs in my living room. The portrait shows her in mourning, with the deceased's locket portrait on her neck.) She then married again, a man who spent all her money. She ended up at the siege of Paris in 1870, when people ate with relish, such was their hunger, the animals in the zoo as well as rats and mice. Great grandmama escaped from Paris in a hay wagon, dressed and acting like a deaf and dumb milkmaid. What she was doing in Paris, I have no idea, but I imagine she must have been some sort of governess. She had had a daughter, my grandmother, from her first marriage, whom she had farmed out to a family in Glasgow, Scotland. I knew their name (and have now forgotten it) when I first went to England and checked, because the whole story sounded so unbelievable. I seem to remember that the Scottish family's descendants vaguely confirmed that my grandmother was living with their forebears in the mid-nineteenth century. My great-grandmother—she of the charming and much admired portrait—then turned up in no less a place than Adrianople in Turkey, now called Edirne, where she opened a pension with some French friends, also unknown to me. My grandfather, who was then working for Turkey's government, came to Adrianople and fell in love with my great-grandmother, who did not return his passion. Instead, she sent to Glasgow for her daughter and married her off to Giacomo Leoni. Needless to say, the union was never a happy one. The only other thing I know of my great-grandmother is that she eventually became a governess to the last sultans of Turkey. Blind, but still mischievous, my mother said, she lived out her last years in a nursing home in Rome run by the Diakonissinen nursing sisters, behind the old German embassy on the Capitol. Strange as it is, the Turkish government paid her pension until she died. She is buried in the Protestant Cemetery in the Testaccio, in

Rome, near the Pyramid, where Shelley and Keats are also buried.

I never knew my mother's parents. Her mother died of tuberculosis in Rome in the late nineteenth century. I don't know where or when her father died, nor where they are buried. My mother was the oldest of five children—herself Maria, then Matilde, Giacomo, Margherita, and Leoncino. Matilde married my Uncle Joseph Frank, a friend of my father's, a German also from near Stuttgart, who later became a stamp dealer. He told me what I know about my mother's family; now that he is dead, I regret greatly that I was not more interested. It appears that my mother was left to provide for her family after her father's death, which she did by giving lessons—in what, I don't know. She did not like her mother and grandmother, and even less so, her sister, my Aunt Matilde. Matilde was a small plump woman with wonderful blond hair and large green eyes, whom my mother considered irresponsible about family obligations. Beautiful, and a perfect bitch, people said of Tante Tilde. Since she and my mother were not speaking to each other, but were curious about each other, they both kept me visiting each other's houses. Both women used to pump me like mad about each other's establishments, which I did not like then or now. Brother Giacomo was no good and had to be shipped off to the United States after he had committed the ultimate disgrace of being dishonest about money—he, an officer! My mother never would tell me what became of him in this country and only said that after their mother's death, he and the family completely lost touch. I never was able even to try to trace him, not knowing where in the United States he went. Margherita, after whom I was named, was my mother's love and as beautiful as her sisters, blue-eyed in a languid Victorian way. She married a Jew (from whom I trace my mother's anti-Semitism), and her husband was apparently horrible, locking her up in the apartment or letting her see only his equally horrible sister. He never went to see Margherita when she was dying of tuberculosis in a hospital, my mother said once to me, adding that she had hated him more than anybody in her life. When I must have been seven or eight years old, my mother and I were in my father's tailor shop near the Tunnel on the Via del Tritone in Rome when a well-dressed middle-aged gentleman came in. My mother seized me by the hand, dragged me up to the man, and said loudly, "This is Margherita, whom I named after my sister, your wife, whom you brutally killed!" and left the shop with me. Leoncino my mother also loved during the five short years of his life. Where he died and what from, again I don't know, but my mother told me that while in Germany on a certain day (why? when?) she knew that he had died on that day. Indeed, her premonition was right.

My Aunt Matilde and my Uncle Joseph Frank, both piously and socially involved with the German clergy in Santa Maria dell'Anima, the church that catered to the pious German Catholics in Rome in those days, are buried in the small cemetery which is part of St. Peter's Enclave in Rome. They stayed in Italy during World War II, but by that time we all had lost touch with each other. When I went back to Rome after the war to see what had happened to my family, I learned that after my aunt died, my Uncle Joseph was living in the large, old-fashioned flat off the Piazza Navona, which I remembered as jammed with furniture and small, unpleasant bric-a-brac that my aunt adored. At the time, there was a desperate shortage of apartments in Rome; thus, after my aunt's death, Uncle Joseph made arrangements with a watchmaker from the South Tyrol, by which the watchmaker and his wife would look after Uncle Joseph during his lifetime and then inherit all his money, apartment, and contents. I wanted to see the couple to find out what had happened and how things had gone with my aunt and uncle. All I learned via the wineshop next door was that the watchmaker and his wife had done very well by my uncle, deserving their inheritance, the man stressed, and that they had gone back to the Tyrol, without ever giving a sign of life to their old friends and neighbors. My uncle was the last person to have known my father and mother, and would have been very willing to tell me about them, had I been interested.

My mother was thirty when she married my father. He was deeply in love with her, as I gather from a book of handwritten love lyrics he wrote for her. But this was not so on her part. Why not, I don't know, but I cannot remember my parents ever sharing a bedroom or being affectionate with each other. I still find it repulsive to consider one's parents as sexual beings, but I imagine my mother did not like sex in general, and closed her eyes to its existence. She had had a long, painful labor in producing me, her only child, and like so many Italian women, she had been greatly disappointed with getting a daughter, rather than a son, for all her sufferings. So she told me every year on my birthday until she died in my New York apartment, aged ninety-two.

What else do I remember of our Roman apartment? A statue of the naked Venus of Milo that stood under the Turkish bronze banister pieces. The life-size lady was chastely and completely covered with bathroom towels when a friend of my father's, an attaché at the German Embassy to the Vatican (known as the Black Embassy), came to visit us. It seems that the young man was so ineffably pious, chaste, and pure that my parents did not want to offend him with so lewd a sight as naked old Venus of Milo.

Opposite us, on the same floor, was the Albanian Consulate, run by the minions of King Zog of Albania, good-looking and well-groomed young men. They used to upset my mother because they kept on flirting with our maids. On the top floor lived the Ciano family, whose son later married Mussolini's daughter and, later still, came to an inglorious end. The Cianos were very poor and lived on father Ciano's modest naval pension. The son, well in his teens, was a sallow youth, and I remember that the two Ciano men shopped for food (an obvious sign of poverty in those bourgeois days) and bought their meat from a horse butcher's shop.

On September 20, 1870, Rome fell to the French troops and the pope no longer ruled. One year on the commemoration of that event, I remember seeing a couple of very bent and very old men wearing red shirts, and being told that these men were the last Garibaldini, who had fought with the great Garibaldi for Italy's freedom. The red shirts were in honor of Garibaldi, who always wore a red shirt on his campaigns.

After Mussolini came into power, his car and escorts passed our house at noon every day on the direct route to his downtown office in the Palazzo di Venezia. And every day, one of his security guards came to all the apartments facing Mussolini's route to make sure that all the shutters and windows were closed tightly for "safety reasons." My father, when he was told of this, said only, "It figures." He was connected with the German Embassy (the White Embassy to the Italian Kingdom) as a diplomatic observer, and he observed specifically the labor problems of the new regime. Besides Goethe, politics was the major interest of his life; only much, much later, when I was already here in America, did I realize that we talked about little else at home. My father, close friend of Ebert, Scheidemann, and other prominent socialist leaders of the Weimar Republic, knew every political personage in Europe. Everybody who came to the house was in politics as a diplomat, as a journalist, or simply as a person. My father went to all the now legendary international conferences after the First World War, very often as a German delegate.

I was an only child but was never treated as a child. It was taken for granted that my parents' interests would be mine. Thus, I never played with dolls or games, and from the age of ten I went by myself to museums, concerts, and lectures, provided they happened in daylight. And I read, read, and read voraciously, whatever book or periodicals I wanted to read; my father's great library was completely at my disposal. Our way of living somehow insulated me from the outside world, though I was a vivacious, loquacious, and open child, given to quick tempers but not to sulking. My mother and I, as mothers and daughters will, frequently got into bad hassles. I remember one especially, when my mother found me with a copy of *La Vie*

Parisienne, a black-fishnet-stockings-oh-la-la publication considered extremely risqué at the time. She put me out of the apartment until I howled that I would never, never again read such filth or ask why the Apollo Varieta was not the place for me to go to see a show. Out of curiosity, as a grown-up and mother, I got hold of an old number of the wicked publication. This was in the mid-fifties, and even then—sex not being as public a matter as it is now—it seemed harmless enough.

My mother was not consistent in her attacks of prudery. She liked taking cures in spas, either to soothe her nerves or to stimulate them, she said. When I was eleven or twelve years old, one Easter she took me with her to a spa in the formerly Austrian part of Italy called the Alto Adige. As Mama took the day-long cure, there was nothing of any kind for me to do except read. But I had brought no books and had to fall back upon the single reading item provided by the hotel, namely, Casanova's *Complete Memoirs,* thirteen large volumes in all. I was a quick reader, and so read each of the thirteen volumes at least twice during the fortnight of my mother's cure. The only part I thought interesting was Casanova's escape from his Venetian prison over the Bridge of Sighs.

In my Roman childhood, visits with school friends did not exist. Unless people were relatives, they did not come to the house for informal occasions. Grown-ups, if men, met in cafés. Ladies met in Babington's Tea Room on the Piazza di Spagna. Formal occasions were celebrated with a *ricevimento,* a reception where, between nine and midnight, ladies sipped a mild liqueur and a coffee and the gentlemen a whisky. And everybody simpered over the dry biscuits that were passed around, my mother said scornfully. Not so in her day, when chintzy hosts rented their ornate cakes, returning those which had not been cut into. If you wanted to be mean, you asked to sample every cake so that it could not be returned. I never knew this to happen at any *ricevimento* I went to.

My Roman childhood was a good one, and I think that it must have formed the tastes of my later life. I was not religious, because, as my mother's Roman saying went, *"Roma veduta, fede perduta,"* or "once you've seen Rome, you've lost your faith."

I loved my parents and our relatives in Monte Porzio, to whom I was sent whenever my parents or my school could not have me. I was also fond of going to the Swiss Alps in the summer with my mother, who adored a "high mountain" and would never consent to staying in a resort less than 4500 feet high up in the mountains; she was the most energetic walker you can imagine. We went to St. Moritz and to the San Bernardino, which my mother and I preferred to St. Moritz; she because it was wilder and I because I could roam around freely, a small cowbell hung around my neck to let people know where I was building dams and making lakes in the glacially cold local torrent. I went back to San Bernardino later in life, but by then it had become a fashionable, tame place, whereas in my childhood there was only one hotel and one inn. The hotel, the yellow Victoria, was a good one, and I agreed then, as I do now, with my mother that nothing in the world beats a good Swiss hotel.

In the Rome of my childhood, the yearly summer *villeggiatura* was most important. *Villeggiatura* translates into a stay in a cool place. Those who had enough time and money to escape the summer heat in the city would do so. One's social status was also determined by the time and length and, especially, by the place of this sacred Roman institution. The richer classes went farther afield, while the less fortunate people spent their *villeggiatura* in one of the hill towns around Rome. The better-class wives went away at least during July and August. Their husbands stayed behind to earn the family's income, and joined their families for a mere two or three weeks in August, either at the seashore or in the countryside. During the month of July, nice people took their kids to the seashore. The Adriatic resorts with their fine, enormous sandy beaches were considered more desirable than the Mediterranean ones near Rome, which in those days catered largely to the humbler Romans who could not afford traveling across Italy to bathe. My mother disliked the seashore, but she subscribed to the Italian belief the sea air was particularly salubrious for the young. Thus, before going to my mother's "high mountains" in August, we spent a few weeks in July in some Adriatic resort like Porto San Giorgio, or San Benedetto el Tronto. What I remember of these *villeggiature* is the inflexible division of the day: one bathed and swam in the mornings and one walked in the afternoons. Since my mother, like all the *signore* of her day, was convinced that sea bathing was extremely debilitating, she forced me every morning, before we went to the beach, to suck a raw egg. I still gag when I think how carefully she punched two little holes at either end of the egg with a pin, and how threateningly she stood over me when, after the daily struggle, I had to resign myself to get that beastly egg down or to miss the beach.

In Rome, I vastly preferred to go the beach with my Uncle Joseph. He was an easygoing man who never forced me to do anything when we took the train to Fiumicino, a grubby little seaside resort on the Mediterranean that has now become Rome's airport. Since my uncle liked to go swimming when the weather was warm enough (unlike the Romans of the time, who shuddered at sea bathing before July), we spent our June Sundays on the beach, swimming and sunning ourselves. Thanks to my Uncle Joseph, I learned to erect a sun shelter with a sheet tied to four poles and to cool our water *fiasco* the ancient Roman way. The *fiasco,* or bottle, was wrapped in a wet towel and hung from a pole so that the sea breezes could cool it from all sides; the system produces a surprisingly cool beverage without refrigeration. When the sun had dried the wet towel around the *fiasco,* we simply poured some more seawater over it. Since we had to bring everything from Rome—sheet, poles, towels—we kept our food simple. Bread, salami, cheese, and a piece of fruit was all we had, eaten whenever one of us felt like eating. All my life, I have been grateful to my Uncle Joseph for showing how little it takes to have a wonderful time on a beach.

For his vacations, my father went to the Tuscan seashore resort of Forte dei Marmi, where his friends had a villa; he always stayed with them. My mother was not pleased because she suspected the worst; quite rightly so, as I found out many, many years later. I did not know his friends and it never entered my mind that he might have taken me with him. My mother, on the other hand, had a friendship with a famous Swiss lawyer from Locarno, whom we called, for obvious reasons (that is, his big nose), "Il Signor Pinocchio." I am willing to swear that the friendship was strictly platonic because she also went, with me, frequently to stay with his mother, who would not have received us had it been otherwise. She and he lived in Locarno, in the Italian-Swiss canton of Ticino.

I remember them so well, he an elegant, monocled, cynical connoisseur of every aspect of good living, his mother the most proper, staid old *grande dame* who ever lived. Once, in my teens, when I asked "Il Signor Pinocchio" how he could bear my mother, with whom I was very angry, he said that she amused him. I also remember that he took a yearly slimming cure somewhere in German Switzerland, where the patients were not allowed to drink any water or wine with their meals. Ah, the garbage of the mind!

My parents traveled a good deal in the summer, and neither they nor I had any use for my going with them. What child likes to be dragged to remote museums and to have to sit still through endless meals, and what grown-up bent upon culture would choose to waste time minding a vivacious child? My mother did not want to leave me at home with the maids, not so much because of what they would do to me as because of what I would do to them when our wills clashed. My mother had me to keep willy-nilly, but she could and would not risk losing maids she had carefully trained and treated well. When my parents went away, the solution of what to do with me was always the same and it always pleased me no end: I would be sent to Monte Porzio to stay with one or the other of our numerous distant relatives. They had plenty of room in their large houses, and anyhow, they lived with so many dependents that one child more did not make the slightest difference to the household. All it meant to whomever I was to stay with was a cot in the room of one of the female relatives and another place set at the table.

Monte Porzio is a very small town in the Alban Hills, some twenty miles from Rome. To give the little town its full name, Monte Porzio Catone was, according to legend, named after Cato the Elder, Marcus Porcius Cato (234–149 B.C.), who had a villa nearby and who is largely remembered for saying to the Roman Senate for three years, *"Cartago delenda est,"* that is, "Carthage must be destroyed." Indeed, Carthage was finally destroyed by Rome in the year 146 B.C., but not before having caused the Punic Wars, Hannibal, and a lot of ancient history.

Frascati was the nearest railroad station to Monte Porzio, and like everybody else in the twenties, we traveled by train. The train to Frascati was sublimely indifferent to timetables. Instead of leaving on time, the *trenino di Frascati* would hoot three or four times, making believe it was going to take off, in order to keep passengers from rioting over the delays. Also, the train did occasionally depart on time, so that no one ever dared come late or go for a cup of coffee.

In Frascati, we transferred to a tram that took us to Monte Porzio in half an hour or so. Monte Porzio clustered on top of an extinct volcano; a long, broad road led up to it from the station at the bottom of the valley. Then there was open land on either side of the road; today, all that land is filled with little villas, because Monte Porzio is now a commercial place, where an enormous, shining new winery makes an innocuous (but tasteless) wine sold as Frascati. It is cheap and it travels well, which the genuine Frascati of the old days never did.

In Monte Porzio my favorite relatives were my mother's distant cousins whom I called Uncle Mario and Aunt Giulia. They had two sons, the lively and wicked Nicola and the quite peaceful Augusterello. Uncle Mario and Aunt Giulia were lively people who talked a lot, and since they invariably took an interest in the people around them (which my parents did not), I loved staying with them. My relatives' house was an old *palazzo* once used, so legend said, by Jérôme Bonaparte, Napoleon's youngest brother, for dallying with the local maidens while visiting his sister, Pauline Borghese. (Pauline's Roman husband, Prince Borghese, owned the still-standing chief *palazzo* of the little town, on the main square, with an enormous terrace that had a sweeping view of the plain and mountains to the northwest.) In those days, the old houses of the town did not have really cold running water, so that the fountain in the main square was *the* place to get the cold water with which we diluted our wine at meals. I loved to be asked to fetch the water; it was the only time I was allowed to get into the hubbub of the main square all by myself; I was even praised for bringing home the town gossip.

My relatives' house faced its rather dusty garden with a corner terrace, its gazebo overlooking the long uphill road from the station. The women of the family and their female friends used to sit for hours in the gazebo, embroidering or knitting, and gossiping about who was coming up the hill from the station, having been to Frascati—or even to Rome. Since Roman wives would not have cared to be too far away from their husbands, but wanted to get out of the Roman summer, Monte Porzio was a popular nearby *villeggiatura* to which husbands could come for weekends before the whole family left for the seashore in August. I remember one Saturday afternoon when one of the assembled *signore,* peering over the terrace's banister, cried out: *"Eccolo!"* and swept out through the garden gate to greet her spouse sweating up the hill, jacket hanging over one shoulder, his straw boater used as a fan.

On the ground floor of the house was the dining room, which overlooked the garden. Uncle Mario was an irascible man when it came to food. When a dish did not suit him, he, like all of his well-to-do friends, simply flung the whole thing out the window into the garden. Since I don't remember ever seeing any of the outcast food among the paths and the flowers, one of the numerous peasant maids must have removed the sordid mess while we ate. The *salone* was also found on the ground floor, a large room with a long, narrow sideboard, displaying a row of ancient Chinese figurines that nodded their heads when you pushed them, a forbidden but frequently indulged-in pastime of the maids and children of the house. As far as I remember, nobody ever went into the *salone;* even the parish priest, who regularly came for Sunday midday dinner, was received in the dining room or upstairs, in my Uncle's study or in the room overlooking the street where he displayed the coins, Roman lamps, pots and shards, and other antiquities that had been dug up in his vast properties of olive groves and vineyards.

Our bedrooms were on this floor and so was the bathroom, the pride and joy of my relatives, who had fitted it out with the works—tub, loo, bidet, sinks (two of them)—imported from Germany, the most fashionable and up-to-date fixtures of the time, all gleaming white. Only one thing was missing—running water. This, however, was no problem in the days of abundant domestic help; Italy at that time was a poor country, where servants could be obtained for pennies. So the maids, taking turns, sat outside the bathroom door, ready to flush toilets with a pail of water and to fetch the water we needed for our frequent ablutions.

Uncle Mario and Aunt Giulia were fond of eating out of doors in an unconventional manner, which now would be called a picnic. Before I describe the most spectacular picnic of my life, let me say that when I was a child, the word "picnic," for out-of-door eating, was not known to us, either in Rome or in Monte Porzio. When in the summer we went out into the countryside to visit the olive groves and the grapevines of one or the other of Uncle Mario's tenants, we took with us the classic standard Italian *panini imbottiti,* unbuttered hard rolls stuffed only with prosciutto or salami. We ate them in the tenant's cool cellar and drank the tenant's wine, cut with water. The wine, in its rustic straw-bottomed *fiasco,* hung, as on the beach, from a pole outside the cellar, to keep it away from the broiling hot sun, and to catch the noonday breezes.

It was all right to eat this informally in the depth of the country. But even in Monte Porzio, and certainly in Rome, *gente per bene,* nice people, would not have dreamed of such an informal behavior as eating out of hands. ("Never, but never, eat anything in the street" was so drilled into me that, to this day, I feel guilty even licking an ice cream cone in the park on a hot summer afternoon or popping a piece of candy into my mouth at a street fair.)

The most spectacular picnic of my life took place on my Uncle Mario's birthday on Tusculum, one of the Albanian hills which we could see from Monte Porzio. On the mountain, too, lie the ruins of the Roman city of Tusculum, where the ancients, including Cicero, built their summer villas to enjoy the shady woods and beautiful views. Legend has it that Tusculum was founded by the son of Ulysses and Circe. Rome and Tusculum feuded for supremacy in the region until Rome destroyed her rival completely in A.D. 1181. The top of Tusculum mountain is now dominated by a giant cross within the ruins of the Roman acropolis. The other Roman ruins included such amenities as a 3000-spectator amphitheater which had been partly excavated, a big fountain and reservoir, and a Roman-paved road. (In spite of a new motor road and modern comings and goings, Tusculum retained its magic, I thought, when I returned there some years ago.)

My Uncle Mario loved Tusculum over every other place in the neighborhood, no matter how picturesque, historical, artistic, and shady, such as the nearby Renaissance Villa Mondragone, which is very famous indeed among Renaissance villas. Mondragone used to be a Jesuit boarding school, and Nicola, Uncle Mario's son, went there until the local Jesuit Fathers could not cope with the rebellious boy any longer, and transferred him to their school in Arezzo in Tuscany. The Arezzo Jesuits were famed throughout Italy for running not only the Order's, but Italy's, toughest boarding school. As it was put in a letter to my relatives, they soon reduced the boy to his just proportions, but, alas, once back home, he was again above himself. My personal memory of Mondragone is that I was never allowed to see any of its exterior and interior splendors for the simple reason that

I was *femmina*, a female, and in those days females were not allowed into that male enclave. I did not mind at all, because when I had to wait at the gates for Uncle Mario, summoned by Father Superior to complain about Nicola's constant infractions, the lay brother who opened the gates used to sit me in the shade of an old oak and feed me sweet wine and biscuits.

On Tusculum we ate near the theater in the deep shade of the ancient oaks and chestnut trees. Our food, packed in baskets, was carried by three maids up the Roman-paved road since, in those days, the motor road did not reach the mountaintop. The dishes, glasses, and flatware were wrapped in snowy tablecloths and napkins and carried in two suitcases. These were then used as tables and spread with the cloths on which we set out our foods. We would have whole chickens, roasted the day before with rosemary sprigs and basted with olive oil and wine, un-carved to preserve their juiciness, and platters of wafer-thin rosy prosciutto and pungent salami. The stuffed eggs, essential to an outdoor meal, were seasoned with a little olive oil and mayonnaise, a dash of fiery hot sauce, and a touch of onion and garlic, each stuffed egg half topped with a little ring of capers. Neatly wrapped hunks of Parmesan and Provolone cheeses were there for the nibbling; so were the unopened cans (to avoid spilling) of tuna fish and sardines and their vegetable mates such as caponata, made with eggplant, sweet peppers, onions, and ol-ives, as well as plain boiled chick-peas, raw fava beans (to be dipped in salt), and fresh radishes. To sustain life even further, we would also have a great baking pan of the classic Roman *pomodori ripieni,* tomatoes stuffed with rice and then baked, which every traveler to the Eternal City has seen in the restaurants. The *filoni* had been picked up from the bakery just before our setting out for the picnic; we could not have eaten without fresh bread.

Of course, we drank on the picnics. First we would toast my uncle with the traditional little glass of sweet vermouth called *il vermut d'onore* and then wash down our food with my uncle's own red and white wine, put up in straw-bottomed *fiaschi.*

For dessert we ate anisette toast, sweet egg cookies, and fruits—sun-warmed figs, apricots, and peaches that we had bought from the peasants on our way to Tusculum. Nor did we forget the Thermos of very strong, very hot, sweet black coffee.

After eating, the maids (who ate with us in a patriarchal manner, sitting a little to the side) removed every trace of the meal. Each one of us would then find his or her own dappled bit of shade, and rest in the still noon of the day. Later we would pick the wild fragrant cyclamen that grew among the ancient masonry, and wander about to look at the Roman *campagna* and distant sea, much as the Romans of two thousand years ago must have done on a summer's day.

How do I now feel about picnics? My idea of a good picnic is when I can fix the food at home and need only to carry and unpack it. No outdoor cooking of any kind for me; if cook I must, I will do it where I am most comfortable myself—in my own kitchen. However, my truer and lower self yearns for exquisite repasts carried by a liveried chauffeur to a bosky glen, where two footmen have set a table with damask, silver, and crystal, and will serve us cook's best galantines, chaud-froids, custards, and raspberries, and lots of superlative hock and Champagne. The footmen are wearing white gloves. But the self that knows the realities of life knows that this dream will never come true (chauffeurs maybe, but footmen with white cotton gloves these days?). Here are a few words of picnic advice from a scarred veteran with a heartfelt sour "picnic if you must":

Let me say at once that I will not tell about cooking uncooked foods out-of-doors over a grill that is fueled by coal, briquettes, or wood. I know that this kind of cooking outdoors has now become a national craze, but I also know that if a body is ignorant about the whole matter, numerous articles and books will tell her/him all. There are two kinds of picnics: the wholly spontaneous one and the planned one. For the first, the hostess gathers whatever foods she can find at the nearest deli, gourmet shop, or take-out, places them in a box with a minimum of accoutrements (napkins are essential, or paper towels) and the

necessary booze, and that's it. For the second, you must first be
sure that your guests really like to picnic (a given with the
spontaneous picnic): be explicit and question them when you
extend the invitation. Always remember that you have invited
people to eat with you and that you have the obligation to
provide food for them at a reasonable time.

If you have decided to have a major picnic, choose a spot that
is easy to get to and to get away from. If the spot involves a
certain amount of walking, you must make absolutely sure that
your guests are willing or able to walk even a few minutes.
Remember that swamps, rising tides, poison ivy, ants, pebbles,
and trespassing notices spoil picnic enjoyment. If your picnic
site is distant or hard to get to, don't fuss with fancy foods, but
take foods that are easy to carry, such as sandwiches, hard-
boiled eggs, hard fruits like apples or pears (these do not bruise
easily), and cookies, apart from the necessary beverages.

For a major picnic, bring a large, colorful cloth to spread on
the ground so that the food can be set out, and have the ladies
decorate it with flowers or leaves found on the spot. (Gathering
the decorations will keep them busy until eating time.) Bring
large napkins with you or use colorful bandannas for napkins.
Don't forget that everybody in the party may not be able or
willing to sit on the ground, so bring a folding chair or two with
you. Good plastic plates are permissible, but plastic flatware is
not. If you don't want to take your own family forks and knives,
good flatware that may be silver, invest in some inexpensive
stainless-steel picnic sets. Personally, I hate to drink from plastic, but plastic glasses are up to you. Also, at home, keep all the
picnic appurtenances in one place for future use.

If you want to heat food, be sure to choose a kettle or casserole that will not crack over an open fire. Many attractive cas-
seroles are made for oven cooking only and won't stand the
direct heat of an open fire. If yours is to be a bird-and-bottle
picnic, carve the bird at home, because it is easier, and wrap
each piece separately. But if you take along a roast, keep it

whole or the meat will dry out. Take a board and a sharp knife, and carve the meat on the spot.

Keep the food hot—or chilled—in insulated containers, or make your own by lining sturdy, deep shopping baskets thickly with about three dozen sheets of newspaper each. Hot food should be placed in a container that can be reheated over an open fire if necessary, and cold food set into a plastic bag filled with ice cubes and covered with a pillow or a cushion you can later sit on. Cover with more newspapers and tie fast. Or use another cooling gadget, the kind of thermal pad that can be chilled overnight (available from all hardware stores).

Carry cheese in a hunk and leave French or Italian bread whole—it dries out very quickly. Fresh fruit is the best picnic dessert, to my mind, with plain cookies or a slab of bitter chocolate. Crackers, guava paste, and cream cheese are also good, but avoid anything creamy that will drip on you or go bad in the sun. Be sure to bring a lemon or two, because lemons are always useful, if for nothing else than to make lemonade with the plentiful, cold water you must also bring along. Water is so often forgotten, but nothing takes its place when you are thirsty.

It is essential that there should be sufficient alcoholic and nonalcoholic drinks, all well chilled, as well as plenty of water. Consume hard liquor with caution, but it is a good idea to dispense one or more slugs of hooch to your guests the moment the site is reached; or serve soft drinks or fruit juices to those who prefer them. This cheers all present and puts them in a good mood while waiting for the food, especially since cooking or reheating food always, always, always takes much longer than one expects. Champagne for starters, followed by light white wine, works very well and is simple to dispense. Rosé wines are nice, too. In any case, figure on at least half a bottle of wine per person and hold some of the same wine in reserve. Don't forget the corkscrew, without which most of your efforts are in vain. Coffee, strong and black, kept hot in Thermoses, is a necessity. Serve milk and sugar separately, always.

If you want to cook outdoors, or if you want to heat food,

bring your own fuel, because firewood may be nonexistent on that heavenly site you choose. Make sure fires are really out, and collect all your garbage; leave it in garbage cans, if they are provided; if not, take it home and get rid of it there.

Finally, do *not* forget: bottle opener, can opener, salt, pepper, cigarettes and matches, paper toweling, knives, forks, spoons, carving knife, garbage bags, insect repellent, and Wash'n Dries.

To come back to Monte Porzio. In my childhood, odds and ends of antique statuary artifacts, and sometimes even complete pieces, were being constantly dug up in Rome and her surroundings, as they had been for centuries. Almost all the landowning families had in their houses little collections of Etruscan, Greek, and Roman fragments, which had been unearthed in their vineyards and olive groves. On Tusculum, for instance, Augusterello and I amused ourselves digging for such things; once on Uncle Mario's birthday picnic I even found an old coin which I gave him proudly for his own collections of classical fragments. Theoretically, all that has been dug up should be turned over to the Italian authorities; in practice, finders—or perhaps better, seekers—are keepers, as we all know from our American museums. However, the exporting of antiques is strictly illegal in Italy and severely punished—if the offenders are caught.

My Uncle Mario had three major interests in life: his olive groves and vineyards, his politics—he had been mayor of Monte Porzio several times and was now a parliamentary deputy—and his collection of little bronze and terracotta Roman lamps, which were displayed in glass vitrines in his study. His father's interests in Roman antiquities must have been the first impulse that got Nicola in the whole mess that I am about to relate.

All of our relatives owned a number of antique fragments, but our bits and pieces could not compare with those of Great-aunt Rosa, who, in her big, square gray house, had quite a collection of these. All of them had been dug up, sometimes as long as a hundred and fifty years ago, in the vast properties she had inherited. The best pieces included a legless torso of a boy; the laurel-crowned, noseless bust of an athlete; and a really exquisite, hardly damaged ivory statuette of a man with an outstretched arm, which through some miracle had not been broken off by the diggers. This statuette was about fifteen inches tall and obviously of Greek origin. It had been found in Aunt Rosa's early youth on a site where there must have stood a Roman villa, to judge from the antique masonry that still is there.

My Great-aunt Rosa had never been particularly interested in her collection because it brought in no money. She was an old miser, and a termagant as well, who devoted all her time and considerable intelligence to getting as rich as she could. Her means were often extremely questionable, but since she planned to leave her fortune to the Church, she felt that the ends justified them. Aunt Rosa, as I called her, was quite frank about her love for money. She said that only three things mattered in a woman's life: love, money, and old age. Since the last had made the first obsolete, she added, she might just as well concentrate on money. I found it difficult to imagine that the tall, gaunt old woman, whose black eyes dominated her face, and who always wore high-necked black dresses, thick black stockings, and elastic-sided boots, had ever felt the pangs of love or its joys. But apparently she had loved her husband and her child, both of whom she had buried many years before. She still wore widow's weeds for them when she went out, and the only ornaments I ever saw her wear, apart from her own and her husband's wedding rings, was a parure of black jet—but this on special occasions only, such as saints' days and on New Year's, when she received her friends and tenants.

From the way Aunt Rosa behaved, it was obvious that her fund of love for others had been exhausted long ago. But she belonged to a generation of the Italian bourgeoisie who could not admit that one might find one's family detestable. She constantly protested her devotion, never forgetting to remind us that her life had been one long sacrifice for a group of people who clung to her like leeches. This in a way was true, because for years and years she kept her inheritance dangling in front of her relatives, who therefore stuck close to her and put up with an incredible number of questionable demands on their persons, their time, and their connections. "Ah well, families must stick together," my relatives would say when Aunt Rosa's latest outrage was discussed. "Else we'll have anarchism." Thus, on both sides, decorum took the place of morality and smoothed over the unavoidable outbursts that happened from time to time.

Nicola was the one member of the family to whom Aunt Rosa gave a certain amount of "confidence," that is, he was intimate enough with her to drop in at her house whenever he wanted to—a thing no one else in the family dared to do. She even spoke on his behalf when complaints about his irresponsibility were brought to her attention. "It is only natural for a boy to play with a gun," Aunt Rosa said, ignoring that Nicola had been taking potshots at his mother because she had offended his honor, so he said. However, when the boy started shooting at the streetlights in Monte Porzio and gunning the tenants' mules, my uncle and aunt realized that this kind of behavior was not furthering his father's career. Since summer camps, that blessed convenience for parents of unruly children, were unknown in Italy, it was decided to give Nicola a tutor and companion who would keep him out of mischief.

The tutor Nicola acquired, and who was there when I came to stay with Uncle Mario and Aunt Giulia that fateful summer, was a young Englishman in his very early twenties called Nigel. Considering the fact that Nigel later became a respectable member of society in England, I will not give his real name. In any case, he was known in Monte Porzio as "Il Lord Inglese." The amiable blond and already slightly balding youth, who dressed in gray flannels, a blazer, and sneakers, was not a lord at all, but merely the younger son of one. Nigel could not go back to England until he had done penance as a remittance man and become more honest in the issue of checks to pay for his wine, women, and song. At Oxford, which he had had to leave under a cloud, he had become fond of the classics and so, instead of going to the parts of the British Empire where remittance men used to congregate, Nigel chose to sit out his exile in Italy and fill his time with a little archaeology.

Nigel had been recommended to my relatives by a honey-tongued bishop who had converted him to Catholicism. (When he returned to England, however, several years later, Nigel became a Protestant again, took an English wife, and lived as if he had never set foot outside the British Isles.) Apart from the bishop's interest, the young man's obvious good manners, his agreeableness, and his interest in archaeology had impressed my uncle. The Roman lamp collection needed cataloguing and this Nigel could do when Nicola went back to his Jesuit boarding school in the autumn.

Nicola and Nigel hit it off immediately. Nicola was impressed and tolerable to have around. Not that he and Nigel were around much; they spent their days roaming the countryside, taking what they called archaeological walks. Nicola was supposed to learn English from Nigel. He never did beyond a number of unprintable epithets, but Nigel's Italian improved immensely; he spoke it with a broad Roman accent.

As a member of the household, Nigel was introduced to Aunt Rosa. At first she had been most unpleasant to him. She told my uncle in Nigel's presence that she considered the whole arrangement a shocking waste of money and a grave danger to Nicola's soul, since she did not trust conversions. But Nigel won her over with skillful, indirect compliments—she would have mistrusted any other. She even showed him her collection of antiquities and told him when and where each piece had been found. Nigel was most interested and respectful, which Aunt Rosa liked.

The summer went on and Nigel and Nicola were at home even less. When they were not taking cultural walks, and these walks now included all-day excursions to Rome—to the museums, they said—the boys were at Aunt Rosa's, studying her antiquities at her invitation. Nicola now went about with a spade rather than a gun, and was seen wherever the peasants were digging up the land, searching for buried treasure. Naturally, his parents were enchanted. My uncle attributed this cultural awakening to his own interest in Roman lamps. Incidentally, my uncle's was a legal collection and he spent more money on it than his wife liked. "Ah, Roman blood will tell in the end," Uncle Mario said, preening himself. "And so will an early cultural environment like the one that flourishes in our home. Nicola has learned to appreciate beauty at home, from the cradle on. Il Lord Inglese merely uncovered what has lain dormant all the time, the way the sun brings out the flowers of spring."

One day my Uncle Mario went to see Aunt Rosa on a business matter, and found the old lady in the room that housed her collection of antiquities. As he looked around, he noticed that a great many of the familiar pieces were missing, such as the boy's torso, the athlete's bust, and, above all, the ivory statuette, which usually was placed in a small vitrine of its own. "What happened to your antiquities?" he asked Aunt Rosa. "The boys have taken them out into the garden because they want to clean them and bleach them in the sun," she replied. "Isn't it nice of them?" "Well, let's hope they are careful with the ivory statuette," my uncle said. "Oh, I know I can trust them," was Aunt Rosa's answer. After this, they went on to business. My uncle repeated this casually at lunch, from which the two lads were absent.

A few days later, my uncle received an urgent telegram as he was about to sit down for lunch. It came from the Questura, the police headquarters in Rome, and ordered him to present himself there in person as soon as possible. The stationmaster, who also ran the Monte Porzio telegraph office, had brought the telegram in person, out of curiosity as to why my uncle, a distinguished member of Parliament and a rich man, should have to go to the police as if he were an ordinary citizen. My uncle, too, was extremely puzzled, and remarked that his conscience was clear, and that his lawyer was perfectly capable of dealing with the matters on which his conscience was somewhat less serene. But he changed rapidly into his city clothes in order not to miss the local trolley that would take him to Frascati, to catch a train to Rome. My aunt, too, was calm and said that there must have been some misunderstanding, but that Uncle Mario should go to find out and clear everything up.

Nigel and Nicola had been out during the morning and came in for lunch with their usual excellent appetite. I remember what we had that day—green spinach noodles and roast chicken and salad. We were just digging into our second helpings of chicken when one of the maids came in, all white and shaking. She whispered something into my aunt's ear, whereupon Aunt Giulia got up and left the room quite visibly upset. Nicola, Nigel, and I went on eating with calm concentration. Then my aunt returned, weeping loudly, "Nicolino, Nicolino," she cried, "and you, Needgel, the *carabinieri* are here to arrest you. They won't tell me why and Papa is not here. They say they don't know anything themselves. But if you don't go quietly," she added, and at that moment Monte Porzio's two local policemen appeared in the dining room looking horribly embarrassed, "they'll make you go by force. You better go with them. In any case, Papa will be back with the evening tram." In silence, Nicola and Nigel got up and left the room with the *carabinieri*. Nigel managed to drain his wineglass quickly first.

We spent an utterly bewildered afternoon. Aunt Giulia went to the police station, but she was not allowed to see the boys. Nor would the chief of police enlighten her. He claimed to know nothing, and that he was merely acting on orders from the Rome Questura. Then my aunt sent for the *arciprete*, the parish priest, and made him go to the police station, but he had no better luck.

The evening tram arrived around six. My aunt and I went to meet it, but my uncle was not there. A little later, a *carabiniere* came to the house to tell her that she could send the boys their supper if she wanted to. He left with two of the maids in his wake carrying baskets full of plates of food, which had been covered with napkins, and two bottles of wine, as well as a clean tablecloth, glasses, knives, and forks. The evening dragged on. I was trying to read and my aunt was telling her beads. The *arciprete*, who had remained with us, was reading his breviary.

Finally, around ten o'clock, a car pulled up by the garden

gate. My uncle's voice was heard as he paid off the driver and wished him a safe journey back to Rome. Now my aunt became truly agitated. "He came from Rome by car, *Arciprete,*" she cried, "he rented an automobile to come home! Such a thing has never happened in our family! *Che disgrazia,* something awful must have happened! God alone knows what. It must be terrible, terrible, for anybody to hire an automobile!" I fully understood what she meant; in those days, I rode in cars twice a year, on New Year's Day and on Easter Sunday, when my father hired a car as an extra special treat. Ordinarily, we went about by trolley or in a rented horse carriage.

My aunt was still wailing when my Uncle Mario came into the room. He threw his hat into a corner and demanded a glass of wine. "Don't go, *Arciprete,*" he said as the priest wanted to withdraw discreetly, "I'll need you to talk [he used a far less polite word] to that old *canaglia* Rosa, since I'm certainly never going to speak to her again."

Then, with much swearing, the story came out. A few days before in Chiasso, a town on the Italian-Swiss border where the customs between the two countries are dispatched, the customs guards—the Italian ones who spot-check the luggage of passengers into Switzerland—had noticed a man acting in a suspicious manner. The train was jammed, and the man, rather than placing a heavy-looking suitcase into the luggage rack above his seat, was keeping it beside him, crowding the other passengers. When asked to open the case, a standard customs procedure, he behaved in an evasive manner. The guards, by now thoroughly suspicious, ordered him and his case off the train and into the customs shed. There they forced him to open the bag. In it there were no clothes, as the man had claimed, but a neat wooden packing case. The guards then gave the man a chisel to pry the case open; this took some time, as the man was very cautious. At last the nails came undone. Hidden under layers upon layers of packing paper was an object, oddly shaped, which was carefully wrapped in cotton. The man, urged on by guards in unmistakable terms, unwrapped the object with trembling fingers. It was an ivory statuette of a man with an outstretched arm, about fifteen inches high, and undeniably a work of art intended to be smuggled out of Italy; the man could show no export papers for it. He was then arrested and taken to the police station. His interrogation showed that he was an antiquarian from Rome, who was going to Switzerland to dispose of the statuette.

The man was taken to Rome the next day and put into prison. He confessed that this was not the first time he had exported works of art illegally. The statuette, as well as some other pieces, he said, had been sold to him by a young Englishman and an Italian boy, who claimed them as their own property. He also gave their names.

It had not been hard at all for the Roman police to trace the father of the boy, since my uncle was well known. But it had been quite hard for my Uncle Mario to talk them out of punishing Nigel and Nicola as much as the antiquarian was to be punished, with a prison sentence. In the end my uncle and the police settled on a stiff fine, and on some favors my uncle did not specify, though he said they would cost him plenty. In return, the police would keep the matter quiet and not give the facts to the newspapers. "It would have meant my career if I had not given in to their demands," my uncle concluded as he drained off another glass of wine.

Then he started shouting, "You know as well as I do who is the owner of the statuette and the other pieces, *Arciprete*. And who put up the boys to selling them. But may I be struck dead by assassins, I am not going to pay the fine. She is going to pay for it, and she is also going to pay every penny this affair is going to cost me. And may her soul rot in hell!"

The *arciprete* did not seem at all pleased at the prospect of facing Aunt Rosa. "Tomorrow, tomorrow," he said. "It's late now, and we must all go to sleep, and thank the Lord that nothing worse has happened." My Uncle Mario laughed at this. "You tell that to that old miser, *Arciprete*," he said. "And you tell her straight after mass. If you don't, I'll sic the police on her. If I am going to suffer, she'll suffer even more." As the priest left the room, my uncle called after him: "The police won't mince words, I assure you. Who knows, she might get a heart attack and I don't think she has made her final will yet. You might not get her money after all!"

"As for the boys," my Uncle Mario then said to Aunt Giulia, "let them sweat it out in jail. It won't hurt them and it might even do them some good. It'll teach them not to sell antiques illegally. Going to the museums in Rome!" and he swore so much that Aunt Giulia kept on crossing herself.

Great-aunt Rosa paid the very stiff fine without a murmur, as the better part of wisdom. She also reimbursed my uncle in a similar manner. The parish priest apparently had managed to convey to her how easily she had come off, thanks to my uncle's position.

It never became quite clear who had started the illegal traffic. The family thought that Nigel was probably aware of the lucrative possibilities lying in Aunt Rosa's antiques, and that the old lady had fallen in with his schemes only too willingly. Neither did we find out what Nigel's and Nicola's profits had been. Uncle Mario thrashed Nicola thoroughly with his walking stick, but the boy did not talk, not then or ever after.

As for Nigel, he remained with my relatives throughout the winter. He catalogued my uncle's lamp collection extremely well, and he also became my uncle's private secretary since his Italian had become excellent. "A more discreet secretary a politician never had," my uncle said with warm admiration.

My uncle and my aunt cut Aunt Rosa dead for several months. Eventually, however, my uncle reestablished relations by going to see her on business and acting as if nothing had happened. "Families must stick together" was his explanation. Once, when I pressed him to tell me if Aunt Rosa really had never mentioned the whole affair, he admitted that she had spoken one sentence. "An unfortunate coincidence," she said, and went on to other things.

As a child and as children will, I took people and their behavior for granted. Now I wish I had paid more attention to the strange things that happened in Monte Porzio among the people we knew, such as the two sisters and a brother who had lived together all of their days in their ancestral *palazzino* not far from Uncle Mario's house. These people lived off the income from their olives and wine grapes, as did our relatives, administering their estates shrewdly, if not too honestly. But since the peasants who worked the estates were also shrewd and not too honest, each side fully deserved the other. The two elderly sisters were animated, small-town Italian women who talked incessantly, frequently contradicting each other, but they were united, and most solidly so, in keeping their brother in his place. He was a tall, wispy, and rather disheveled man, who never spoke; even as a child I noticed his continuous silence in all but the most direct matters. He worked very hard and never seemed to do anything but work or go to church.

All the local people admired him and envied his sisters, who kept the poor man under strict control at all times. He had to account to them for every minute of his time, telephone if he would be so much as five minutes late returning home, and send a messenger if he was delayed by his work in the vineyards and olive groves. His bedroom could only be reached by passing through his sisters' bedroom, so that even during the night he was virtually a prisoner. Well, that was the way things were in that family, and Monte Porzio shrugged its shoulders and thought no more about it.

The man died rather unexpectedly, and then the bombshell exploded as he was being buried. Along with most of the town's inhabitants, my aunt and uncle and I went to the cemetery to toss a handful of earth onto the grave of the honored dead. I was about to do this when an Amazon of a woman, dressed in deepest mourning, her face veiled, surged forward, dragging a little boy by either hand. She looked and acted like Cornelia, the mother of Gracchi, about whom I had just learned in school. "Halt," she said in loud tones, "and let my little boys stand by their father's grave, for who is more entitled to it than my boys?" The enormity of this was such that even the two sisters, dressed all in black but not in widow's weeds, retreated before the unknown woman. She and her boys then knelt before the grave, praying in an ostentatious manner for the soul of the dead man, and praying even louder for his relatives who had made him so unhappy during his lifetime. The funeral ended in shambles. The woman in her deep mourning retreated, dragging the two little boys with her.

She was what she had claimed to be: the deceased's legitimate widow and the rightful heir to his share of the properties, which were considerable. She got them, too, taking his sisters to court and handling the case so skillfully that they agreed to pay up.

How had the brother managed to acquire a wife and children, guarded as he was by his sisters? He had found a shrewd and willing peasant to dally with when he was working in the vineyards and olive groves. He had married her in the nearby town of Rocca Priora, where both parties were unknown, finding an acquiescent priest to complete the civil ceremony; their documents were in perfect order. I cannot say that anybody was sorry for the sisters in Monte Porzio; general sympathy was shown to the legitimate widow. However, she did not come to live in our little town, but remained in nearby Frascati, in a nice little house, where curiosity took me to see her years later. All she would say about his case was: *"Ah, signora mia, bisogna saper fare,"* that is, "you have to know how to do things."

2. MILAN

$\mathcal{W}$hen we moved to Milan, gone were the days when so many of Italy's well-known journalists and politicians came to our house to talk politics with my father. Thinking back, I am sure that by and by he lost his interest for what was going on in Italy now that Mussolini was firmly in place. Also, I am sure that he minded not being able to go as often as he wanted to discuss politics with his Berlin political friends. My father was now a German Consul and a regular civil servant with definite duties, and the world around him had changed with Mussolini's new Italy.

I loved Milan from the moment I set foot in the city, Italy's undisputed financial and business capital. Most of all I loved that Milan, unlike Rome, was not and has never been attractive to tourists. There were plenty of museums, churches, palaces, and quaint streets to see, but they had to be sought out rather than being presented to the visitors on a platter as they are in Rome. Of course, the *divina*, the great Gothic cathedral of Milan, the third largest church in the world, in the center of the city, and the Scala opera house, connected with the Piazza del Duomo by the famous glass-topped Milan Galleria, as well as the fierce Sforza castle of the despot dukes of Milan, are so much part of the city that the Milanese hardly notice them any longer. Indeed, Milan belongs to the Milanese, who are proud and businesslike and rather snobbish in their attitudes to the rest of Italy.

In Milan, I discovered the pleasure of hearing opera by going to La Scala all by myself whenever I felt like it. I heard all the famous singers of the period—Gigli, Tito Schipa, Galli-Curci, Toti dal Monte—and I heard Toscanini conduct standard operas many times. My father used to say that the Maestro's talents lay in killing off the boring parts of old operas so that the work in question would sound new and fresh. How well I remember standing with a large crowd of eager but poor operagoers behind the closed Scala side door, from where one ran as fast as one could up a very long flight of steep stairs that led to the very last gallery just beneath the opera house's ceiling, which was known as *Il Paradiso.* There you could get good standing room for very little money, provided you came early and ran upstairs really fast. I was good at both, and managed to see all that happened on the stage, miles below me, even though it was as if I were looking through the wrong end of a telescope. My parents also liked opera. They always took me with them to see, from an orchestra seat, how poor Parsifal, in the second act of the opera, did not yield to the first two sets of dancers because they were rather old for their trade, but showed visible pleasure at the third and last set of young and pretty ballerinas from the Scala's ballet school. From my orchestra seat, I also saw the two rocks, on which Tristan and Isolde sang their hearts out in act one of the opera, collapse under the weight of the two majestic singers, and how Melchior, a weighty Lohengrin if ever there was one, waited in vain in act three for his boat to take him away because his wife had dared to ask him about his homeland. To this day, I wonder if in any opera there is as much quarreling going on constantly as there is in *Lohengrin.*

Wagner was not only my parents' and my own favorite composer. In Italy, every opera house sports at least one bar where people can refresh themselves during intermission. My father knew Gino, one of the bartenders very well, because he had done him some favor or other. Thus, having repaired during intermission to his favorite bar, my father said to Gino that he loved Wagner better than Puccini. "So do I," said Gino. Surprised, my father wanted to know the bartender's reason for his musical preference. "Well, Signor Console," said Gino, "I don't have to wait for intermissions to fill my bar; during a Wagner opera they are here all the time, and drink like fish. I like Wagner because I make much more money with him than with Puccini."

I can't remember why my parents had to put up Richard Strauss and his wife in our apartment when the composer first came to Milan to conduct at La Scala. His wife, a rather dumpy Austrian actress who was aggressively protective of her husband, had insisted to my mother that Herr Strauss had to follow a special diet and that she expected my mother to provide it for him. My mother, who could not understand why a rich composer did not go to a good Milan hotel, did not like Frau Strauss. Neither did I, because I had to go shopping with her. The unfortunate lady had read somewhere that in Italy you always bargain about prices whenever you want to buy something. This she did invariably in the elegant shops she patronized, telling the salespeople, who could not care less, that they should be happy to wait on the wife of a man invited to conduct at La Scala. My mother, however, got the last word on the food of our unsociable guest, who spoke only to his wife and never to any of us. She provided Herr Strauss with the vittles he could eat to the extent of serving two meals at a formal dinner party for Milan's top political and artistic authorities. One of the dinners consisted of Herr Strauss's pallid vittles (insipid bouillon in a cup, boiled fish with boiled carrots and potatoes, and applesauce) served to him and his wife while my mother explained loudly why the two ate differently and so much worse than their co-guests. These were treated to a sumptuous repast of salmon mayonnaise, breaded turkey breasts (the *clou* of the best Italian dinners), accompanied by delicious little Brussels sprouts, no larger than a small child's thumbnail, and a wonderful vanilla ice cream bombe filled with fresh raspberry purée, created by a famous Milanese confectioner.

In Milan I started becoming more conscious of my surroundings. Oddly enough, the climate had quite a lot to do with this. In Milan the summers are very hot, though the winters are cold and snowy, and above all, misty. I loved the mist, and on those foggy days I took long walks all by myself through the city. I shall never forget how the mist swirled around the buildings so that one never saw them as a whole.

I feel lucky to have known the eighteenth-century and early-nineteenth-century parts of the city, of which only a few streets exist today after the Allied bombings in World War II. The Via del Gesù, the Via della Spiga, and all the other narrow, cobbled little streets not far from La Scala transported one back to the Milan Stendhal describes in his *Chartreuse de Parme* (which, by the way, is a great book). They were silent streets, with odd little shops, such as the one kept by two old ladies who embroidered exquisite white blouses when they felt like it. Today, these old streets have become fashionable, and the architecturally finest of them are lined with the most fashionable and expensive antiquarians and boutiques of Milan.

The courtyards of the big *palazzi* charmed me especially. In the summer, their luxurious gardens filled with flowering trees and big, colorful flowers beckoned through the enormous portals of the great house. Seen piecemeal through the fog, the gardens looked even more romantic.

I loved walking in the old parts of Milan in the late autumn, when the dense white mists for which the city is known enveloped the shabby eighteenth-century houses. And I loved the haunting aroma of chestnuts simmering in vanilla-flavored sugar syrup that wafted out of dark basements where small family enterprises transformed the season's chestnut crop into *marrons glacés*, to be sold later in Milan's pricey *confiseries*. To become a *marron glacé*, a chestnut must be large, perfectly shaped, and without a blemish. But chestnuts crumble all too easily during their transmogrification, so that it was possible to buy the sweet crumbs for a few pennies. Whenever I could, I would get myself a bagful of *marrons glacés manqués*, and eat them while I strolled in the mist that shrouded me like a gigantic cocoon. In the *confiseries*, each candied chestnut sat in its own frilly little paper cup, with passionate candied violets scattered among them to set off their glossy, sugar-streaked surfaces. Sold by weight, they were lifted out tenderly from their display cases, carefully weighed on the scales, and packed into a flat carton tray, along with a few of their mates, the candied violets. (I still think that *marrons glacés*, which must be freshly made or else they are dry, are the best of all possible sweetmeats.)

In Milan, I also started reading any book I could lay my hands on. There were thousands of volumes in my father's library, which was open to me without reservation, filled with German, Italian, French, and English classics, and with the German translations of Russian works. (According to my father, English and Russian translated very well into German.) Dostoyevsky was my favorite author, whose *Idiot* I reread many times, as I did Chekhov and Pushkin. But I must confess that, to this day, I have found Tolstoy's *War and Peace* so excruciatingly boring that I have never read more than fifty pages of it, though I am fond of his *Anna Karenina*.

My mother was seldom interested in what I read. But once she took her hairbrush to me and whacked me really hard. I could not understand why, but I discovered that she had found in my room two books by Guido da Verona and Pitigrilli. These two now-forgotten writers were considered audacious, salacious, and generally wicked beyond words. Since I never had a chance to look at those fountains of wickedness, I could not understand my mother's anger. A great many years later, by chance I came across a book by Pitigrilli. I found that it told of rich gentlemen canoodling with ladies who wore only black net stockings and lacy garter belts and who sighed while canoodling away. Guido da Verona's popular opus was called *Mimi Bluette, Fior del mio Giardino.* But I never found out what Mimi Bluette, Flower of my Garden, did, because I had totally forgotten about her. Too bad!

I don't remember the exact date when my father took me with him on his yearly visit to Gabriele D'Annunzio. The poet-soldier had now become part of Italy's political and literary past, but until his death in March, 1938, he was, with his friend Mussolini, famous in Europe beyond belief. D'Annunzio was a great sailor and airman as well as a poet and a *viveur,* and his 1919 occupation of the city of Fiume (now in Yugoslavia) had created a sensation greater than Nixon's Watergate. D'Annunzio's literary fame was based upon his marvelous use of language in his flamboyant poetry and novels. He was a womanizer (to put it mildly) and proud of his passionate way with women. The most famous of his affairs was his liaison with Eleonora Duse, the great Italian actress, whom he treated so badly that he broke her heart. (Such was the power of Duse's stage presence that I have been told repeatedly that simply by standing still on the stage and looking sad she would make even strong men weep.) As I am writing this, I have reread D'Annunzio's best-known novel, *Il Fuoco,* which describes his love affair with the actress, and I have dipped again into his lyrics. His language may be very flamboyant, but now that flamboyance is coming back into fashion, I daresay that D'Annunzio's writings will be resurrected.

How my father became friendly with the "Comandante," as D'Annunzio liked to be called, I do not know. But the great man's annual invitation stated specifically that he was to bring me along on the next visit to Gardone Riviera, on Lake Garda, where the soldier-poet lived in retirement in his villa. Needless to say, this invitation meant a great deal to both of us.

We took a train to Gardone early in the morning and arrived at noon; Gardone is but a couple of hours from Milan. D'Annunzio had created for himself a vast, flamboyant complex called

Il Vittoriale, with a neglected garden surrounding the prow of a battleship that stuck out into the waters of Lake Garda. We wasted no time looking at the extraordinary Byzantine contortions of the Vittoriale building, but went straight to D'Annunzio's actual dwelling, called the Priory. The house had originally belonged to a German Wagnerian expert, and it had been requisitioned from him after the First World War. I was far too excited to notice what the house looked like; all I remember is that inside, on the walls, on the doors, and wherever there was any room left by the hundreds of knickknacks, photographs, and other luxurious paraphernalia, there were religious inscriptions from and about Saint Francis of Assisi. D'Annunzio, in his old age, became religious, and he was an intense admirer of the saint. However, he did not feel it necessary to carry out his admiration by renouncing his worldly goods as Saint Francis, known as "Il Poverello" (the poor little one), had done so many centuries ago.

It turned out that, notwithstanding our specific invitation, we had come on the wrong day. The servant who opened the door was dressed in the brown Franciscan habit, with bare, sandaled feet. Holding a finger to her lips to ensure our silence, she conducted us to the *officina,* a large workroom filled with so much stuff, including several encyclopedias, papers, and maps, that it felt claustrophobic. There we waited for an eternity. Finally, D'Annunzio himself came into the room, dressed also in a brown Franciscan habit, with bare, sandaled feet. He shut up my father's introductions by holding a finger to his lips, and by not speaking one single word to us. Instead, he led us through convoluted dark passages to the dining room, which was so dark that all I could distinguish were the heavily curtained windows and a profusion of cushions scattered around. In utter silence, we sat down at a bare table laid with only a spoon. (In those days, one always ate from a tablecloth, and table mats had not yet been invented.) Thus the poet, my father, and I sat in utter silence in the dark and stuffy room. Finally, a maid, also dressed as a Franciscan brother, brought each of us a glass filled with water, and one cold egg that sat in an egg cup. No salt, no bread came with it. We ate our eggs in total silence. The poet got up from the table and left the room, again without uttering a word. Then the maid came in again, and informed us that this day, being one of abstinence, one egg was all the lunch we would get, and that since the Comandante had retired for the day, we might just as well leave the place since we would not see him again. With these words she went out of the room, leaving it to us to find our way to the front door.

When we arrived home in Milan so very much earlier than expected, all my mother said was, "What else would you expect from a charlatan like D'Annunzio?"

However, the Guido da Verona episode had reverberations. All of a sudden, so it seems from my faulty memory, my parents got concerned about my education. Rightly so, I think, because I needed some systematic schooling and I did not have any after Rome.

The matter was brought to a head with the *marrons glacés* and *ricevimenti* affairs. Both have influenced me for life; I love *marrons glacés* and, as in Rome, I loathe *ricevimenti,* that is, receptions of any kind, and I sincerely hope that the strictly social receptions, as perpetrated in my Italian youth, have died a natural death. A reception took the place of a cocktail party, but it was very different from the bibulous goings-on of American affairs I have attended. A *ricevimento* began around ten o'clock at night, with refreshments as sparse as they were dignified. First of all, espresso in tiny cups, handed preferably by a white-gloved waiter, was partaken of by everybody. Then gentlemen were offered a choice of whisky (which was always Scotch) and lighter drinks like Campari. The ladies, on the other hand, were shielded from such liquid strength. They sipped liqueurs, which often were violet or pink in color, and they were offered little sweets like chocolate or, when in season, *marrons glacés.* Everybody was dressed up to kill, the men in their best dark suits, the women in afternoon dresses that were as elaborate as they could be. At a respectable *ricevimento,* vapid conversations

65

as well as pallid compliments were exchanged in a genteel manner. The air was filled with boredom, but it was unheard of not to put in an appearance at the reception at a friend's house or, even more importantly, at an official one given by an elevated public personage in the salons of the town hall or an equally official place. My father's position as a consul made it necessary for him and my mother not only to go to but also to give such parties, to pay off social obligations and show that the Germans knew how to behave properly. When a *ricevimento* was given at home, the young people of the family were supposed to make themselves agreeable to the guests and hand around sweets and cigarettes. In our family, it was taken for granted that I would do just that and get out of the way in general, since I was too young to take part in the conversations. Once, to my parents' horror, there were none of the *marrons glacés* left, which I was supposed to hand around for the guests. Why? I had eaten the two kilos my mother had bought for the occasion; in short, I had consumed about 4½ pounds of *marrons glacés,* compounding my sin by not feeling ill after the debauch. Nothing was said about it at the time, however, and the guests may have thought my parents stingy for not offering them the season's customary *marrons,* but otherwise the evening dragged to its languid end. To my surprise, my mother did not speak of my greed the next morning. But when my father came home in the evening, all hell broke loose.

Most of our lives centered around the German Consulate and the German House. The German Consulate was then located in a large bourgeois villa, a leftover from the days when Milan's rich still could build such places with large gardens not far from the center of the city. Since I hardly ever went to the Consulate, all I remember about it is that when the villa was being readied for its consular purpose, it was found that its single bathroom contained a thunderbox which, when weight was put on its arms, played the official Italian national anthem.

We lived in a large, somber apartment not far from the city's center. I remember my father coming home for dinner every night at eight-fifteen. He'd left his job around six and taken his daily turn walking to the Mondadori bookshop in the Galleria to look at the new books and have a learned discussion about books, politics, and, I imagine, life in general with his close friend Mr. Rilke, the bookshop's manager, a German-Italian who was distantly related to the poet.

The Deutsches Haus was subsidized by the German government to give the strong German colony in Milan a social home and to keep an eye on them at the same time. It was said that over fifty thousand Germans worked in Milan, in all sorts of businesses and occupations. Some of the top members were very rich, representing the most important German industries like Bayer and I. G. Farbengesellschaft. Other members were very humble, working as German correspondents in Italian firms, or worse, teaching German to Italians who saw the necessity of learning that difficult language, but still did not make any real efforts to master it. The German elite, and I did not know any other members of the German House, lived in a tight circle, with no social connections among the Milanese. It is extraordinary how little rancor they encountered among the Italians, possibly because the Italians felt they needed the quality goods produced by these firms; I am thinking of the I. G. Farbengesellschaft dyes, the decaffeinated coffee, Haag (which became synonymous with the beverage as Bayer had become with aspirin), the excellent shoe polish made by Kiwi—all products which prospered in the Italian post-World War I market.

The wives of these Germans were good German women who dressed in good-quality clothes; one knew them immediately to be dutiful wives and excellent housekeepers. Two of the ladies I remember best were the red and the black Mrs. H., distinguished by the color of their hair. The red Mrs. H. was a peaceful, somewhat dull soul, and universally liked. But the very fashionable and very thin black Mrs. H. was the envy of all the ladies and the favorite of their husbands. How she kept up her svelte, non-Germanic figure was no secret because she

herself would tell you it was done by a tapeworm in her innards.
I remember the black Mrs. H. telling my astonished parents that
she had come to the conclusion that a tapeworm alone would
keep her trim without having to sacrifice all the rich goodies and
cakes that she loved. So, having procured a very young and
small tapeworm from I don't know where, she swallowed it with
a drink of water and became thin in a short time. All I know
is that the tapeworm never cramped the black Mrs. H.'s style,
nor did it harm her health.

Both the red and the black Mrs. H. admired my father greatly.
As experienced wives, they knew that a man's heart can be
reached remarkably often through his stomach, even when the
man is not one's husband. Thus, both of them put themselves
out to make, for my father, the home-baked goodies of Germany,
which my mother did not know and despised anyway. His favorite, plump *Pfannkuchen* (doughnuts), filled with lush raspberry
jam before baking, and delicately fried *Spritzkuchen* (fritters)
were frequently delivered by a maid. These fragrant gifts came
wrapped in snowy towels so stiff with starch that the sugary
surfaces of the cakes were untouched.

The most interesting representative of Germany's industry
was the Mohwinkel family. While old "Papa" Mohwinkel remained a German, his two sons were of Italian nationality,
which did a lot to facilitate their business dealings. Franz, the
older of the two sons, was a kind, large, but unattractive man,
who later on, when Italy, having lost the war along with the
Germans, was torn with internal strife between the Fascists and
non-Fascists, was killed by the local partisans; it was claimed
that he had been a Fascist. Teddy, his younger and very good-
looking brother, survived and prospered once more, as I was
told some twenty years later. At the time I am writing about, the
Mohwinkel family were the undoubted leaders of Milan's German colony. Papa Mohwinkel, an austere man of few words,
owned a rather large and very austere villa on Lake Maggiore,
where he was apt to invite his social German equals for a day's
outing. I still have one of the menus printed on fine paper with

the photo of the plain Mohwinkel villa. Knowing how much the Germans like to eat, I can't help being astonished at the simplicity of the food. After a clear soup served with cheese straws, the main course was a grilled lake trout served with boiled potatoes, followed by cheese and fruit.

The Deutches Haus fulfilled the functions of a club without many facilities. There was a canteen dispensing *Wurst* and beer, but neither my father nor his friends ever went anywhere near it. They were not by any means above *Wurst* and beer, those cornerstones of popular German gastronomy, but they did not care for the rough-and-ready goings-on of the canteen, preferring to eat in one of the private rooms of the Deutsches Haus. The canteen of the Deutsches Haus employed a good German cook who would prepare complete German meals for my father and his friends. Their "men only" gatherings were called *Herrenabende* (gentlemen's evenings); when the *Herren* ate and drank themselves silly. The food consisted of gargantuan helpings of *Kraftbrühe,* a very strong bouillon, followed by a plainly but carefully cooked juicy pork or veal roast and roast potatoes accompanied by a rather perfunctory green vegetable, and ending with a luscious custard dessert smothered with whipped cream and blistering strong hot coffee. The *Herren* drank a great deal of German wine as they ate, preferring the big wines of the Rhine and Franconia. And inevitably, as the evening progressed, they lifted their hoary voices in songs praising such alien subjects as the free life of the road and the love of a beautiful miller's daughter, and drank beer, and more beer. And, full of beer, they toddled home to their unamused wives who, like my mother, hated those *Herrenabende.*

I can still hear my mother complaining that it was her duty to accompany my father to the Deutsches Haus to help him represent the country he worked for, and who paid him for it, as he would end up telling her with great exasperation. So my mother went along with him because she knew just how much she could exasperate my father. If she liked the company with whom she had been forced to spend the evening, she could and would be absolutely charming. When she did not like the guests, my mother, always a staunch, unyielding anti-Fascist, would speak loudly against Mussolini's regime, a very poor thing to do in those days, especially when one thinks of my father's official position. To annoy him further, she would forbid him to drink and say loudly to whoever was refilling my father's glass with imported and newly fashionable Scotch or with wine, *"Mein Mann dankt,"* meaning a definite "no" to further libations. My father liked his drink and did not mind who knew it. My mother hated to see even the slightest lurching and did not mind who knew this. (I agree with my mother, hating any sign of drunkenness. Living in America, where being sloshed is not considered a cardinal sin, I have been confronted with behavior no Italian would tolerate.)

I was too young to go to the dinner parties in the Deutsches Haus, but I was allowed to go to a few of the dances that were held there regularly. At one in Carnival, I wore a costume of an innocent country maiden, consisting of a long purple dress, a straw hat, and thick blond straw plaits hanging over each ear to simulate golden locks. Needless to say, the costume turned out to be a disaster. Talking of costume carnival parties, I had a great success at one (held in the Scala theater a few years later), dressed as an accurate reproduction of Titian's famous portrait of his daughter Lavinia, whom I resembled. The costume was made of Scalamandré silks, as authentic a reproduction of historical fabrics as they were expensive. I looked smashing and felt smashing, a feeling I have seldom had in my whole life. But the innocent country maiden represented far more my real self. I was indeed both innocent and ignorant at the time. Now I realize that both qualities shielded me, as they do when they are genuine. But I still do not know if they are desirable, and I can't help feeling that a little more knowledge of the ways of the world would have been useful to me then and later on.

Had I known a little more about the ways of the world, I would not have been so shocked when I discovered erotica in a library I was cataloguing when I was about fourteen years old.

One of my father's friends had died, and it was necessary to catalogue the books in his large library. In order to do my father a favor, the family of the rather well-known deceased tycoon had arranged for me to do the job, which consisted simply of writing down the titles, authors, publishers, and dates of the books. Standing on a ladder to get at the top shelf of one of the bookcases, I found that behind the first row of technical volumes there were dozens of well-thumbed volumes describing in words and pictures most unusual sex practices. Perhaps they were not so unusual after all, but I, who barely knew the basics of the subject, thought so. Most of the books were illustrated in the Japanese manner. But I spent no time perusing the strictly forbidden; I only wanted to hide the shameful discovery from the widow of the deceased, a good friend of my mother's. So I rushed home, falling from my ladder in my haste, which netted me a later concussion. My mother was as horrified as I was at my discovery, since we both had been looking up to the deceased as a model of domestic probity; in those days graphic sex was not what it has become today. My mother got my father to come home immediately to deal with this terrible situation. He in turn notified the male members of the deceased's family. They must have removed the books, because nothing more was ever said of the affair. If the widow knew about it, I cannot say.

My memories of our Milan life are not chronological. We changed apartments and went to live on the top floor of a very modern building in one of the newer parts of town. The new apartment was very light and spacious; we even had an extra bathroom with a tub for the maids and for washing the laundry as well. Laundry was dried, sheets and all, in the time honored fashion of Italian apartment dwellers: on ropes running between the windows, the laundry dripping into the courtyard. In the usual Italian fashion, our middle-class apartment house was built around a *cortile,* a paved courtyard. The porter's children played in the *cortile;* the maids in the apartments around it kept up shouted conversations with the porter's wife, the *portiera* (or concierge of French houses); delivery boys rested there before getting their stuff to its destination on foot since only the *signori* and their friends were allowed to use the elevators; repairmen worked there, including the man who stuffed our mattresses with fresh horsehair every third year—much to the envious admiration of the *portiera,* who could not afford a horsehair mattress; hers were filled with something called "kapok," a vegetable fiber given to lumping, she told my mother.

At this time, I began to be conscious of cooking smells. I noticed that the courtyards in Milan smelled differently from those in Rome. In Milan, the smell was largely of reheated coffee and burning butter, whereas in Rome the musty odor of simmering meat soup filled the air all the year round. This soup was *il brodo,* a bouillon made invariably from beef and chicken bones, and occasionally, with a piece of meat, *il bollito,* thrown in. The large *brodo* pot also held a peeled onion, a little celery, and a carrot to make the broth more palatable. However, clarifying the *brodo* with the customary egg whites was never done, nor was it skimmed during cooking as carefully as any meat soup should be.

The insidious odor of the broth permeated not only Roman courtyards but apartments and streets as well. Yet there was no shaking the Romans' belief, including my mother's, in its curative and generally restoring qualities. Yet, in spite of the broth's effluvia, cooking smells in middle-class homes such as ours were considered low class. To this day, I loathe them with a vengeance.

Mercifully, modern progress has done away with the everlastingly brewing *brodo* pot. In its stand, the *dado,* the bouillon cube, has taken over Italy's kitchens; it can be used with a clear conscience since even cookbooks advocate its use. Perhaps bouillon cubes will never be full substitutes for *il brodo,* but they certainly save time and abolish the sickening smell of *il brodo* that plagued me in my Roman childhood. Granted, *il brodo* makes a much better soup, but bouillon cubes do fine for cooking. Talking of bouillon cubes, I am all for the big, flavorful

European cubes, which I have found vastly superior to our American ones.

In Milan I began to become interested in food. What started me on this lifelong interest is that what we now ate tasted different from what we had eaten in Rome. Rather than tasting olive oil in stews, sauces, and sautéed meats and vegetables, I now tasted butter. Only years later, I realized that the basic flavor of any cuisine depends on the fat used in basic food preparations. Milan used butter because the town lay in a part of Italy where dairy cattle could graze on the verdant pastures of the cool regions of northern Italy. In hot southern Italy, the native olive tree prevailed, and, thus, Rome and anything below the Eternal City was olive oil country.

Beyond this simple division, Italy's regional food has been influenced by her history. Etruscans, Romans, Arabs, Lombards, Goths, Normans, Spaniards, French, and Austrians—all Italy's conquerors for a certain amount of time—have left their mark on the foods of the regions they conquered. In the northern parts, where the French and the Austrians once ruled, we find food that is easy on herbs and tomatoes and subtler and more varied than that of the country's southern parts. In the south, the food reflects that of Greece. In Sicily, we find that food is still Arab-influenced, notably in the absence of pork. But the use of pork and its fat, lard, is pronounced in the center of the country, in Rome and in Tuscany, where first the Etruscans and later the Romans dominated. Bread, essential to all Italian eating, was made possible by the Romans, who were large-scale wheat growers.

Italian cooking is more-or-less cooking, based upon the ingredients at hand. The same dish may be called by different names even within the same region, tasting a little different each time, depending on the way it was put together and seasoned. Finally, all of Italy is one great vineyard, and wine is not only a drink, but part of the country's daily food.

The new maids my mother had found locally, as soon as she

had an apartment in Milan, were also responsible for making our food buttery rather than oily. They shied away from eggs and meats cooked in oil, and they vastly preferred rice, the local basic starch, to Rome's pasta. Unlike their rustic Roman counterparts, they did not know the first thing about making home-made pasta, never having to make the most of a handful of flour, water, and an occasional egg. But they were much cleaner and more orderly than their counterparts in Rome, my mother said.

In our new apartment (the house and everything in it was finally destroyed by the Allied bombings of Milan in 1943), my mother had presented me, or rather my room, with a new girlish white and pink bedroom set, which was not to my taste. Her salon consisted of elegant Louis XV furniture upholstered in green damask silk and a piano. The large dining room had framed photographs of the Sistine Chapel, the Coliseum, and the Forum Romanum on the walls, and a six-foot-long eighteenth-century print of Rome, now in my American living room, hung over the sideboard. The sideboard shelf was filled with an enormous silver tea and coffee service, which was used for special occasions. The two good-sized silver pheasants that used to be the formal table decorations of a well-to-do family also stood there. (Many, many years later, when I was writing my Belgian cookbook, I was pleased to find similar silver pheasants in the houses of some Belgian friends.) In my father's study, the one wall without bookshelves was closely hung with the Piranesi prints that still grace my and my son Julian's apartments. Many of the rich Germans' apartments were much grander, furnished with heavy carved furniture, velvet, and damask, but as my parents said, the thousands of my father's books showed that we were infinitely more cultured than they, which they freely admitted.

My father flourished in this new apartment. My mother gave in to all his wishes, which included having in a woman who washed his shirts and another who ironed them since our maids' laundry did not please him. His shoelaces were ironed daily, after the maids had polished his shoes to an unnatural shine (I found out that this was achieved with a lot of spit). As I mentioned earlier, his daily newspaper, fetched early by one of the maids, also had to be ironed free of any folds before he would look at it. All this took place before eight o'clock in the morning, when my father breakfasted on *café au lait* and fresh rolls with butter and strawberry jam. I remember also the fuss caused by my mother's trips to Rome and Switzerland. When the trips were short, my mother told the maids over and over again how the *signore* wanted to be served. But when she went away for a month and more in the summer and the maids also went home, my father was left alone in the apartment. His meals were no problem, what with the splendid Milan restaurants he could now frequent without my mother's remarks about extravagance, not to mention the lavish entertainments of his friends, but there remained the problem of breakfast. My father was totally unable to do anything for himself except shave (which he did every morning with such great good spirits that it was an ideal time to get favors from him, as he stood in front of the mirror, one eye closed, and always with a cigarette hanging from the corner of his mouth, covered thickly with Yardley's Lavender Shaving Cream, his passion, along with an ample dousing of 4711 Eau de Cologne). Leaving behind her maidless and thus helpless husband, my mother had an expensive and complicated arrangement with the super's wife, the *portiera*, by which the woman came up to make my father's coffee and bring him his breakfast. Besides, the *portiera* fetched his breakfast rolls fresh from the baker and brought up his already ironed newspaper. (I don't know about his shoelaces . . .)

My father was wildly popular with whomever he came in contact. He had the charming habit of saying to me out of the blue, "Let us go shopping and take a couple of your friends along." Naturally, I obeyed him with alacrity, and after treating us girls to ice cream in one of Milan's elegant cafés in the Galleria, he bought each of us hankies and similar trinkets, without ever questioning our tastes or our choices. Or else he took me to his tailor, Signor Grandi, to have that wonderful man run up a coat for me, or simply to be there when he was trying on a new suit. My father was a very well turned out man, with a great eye for the more sophisticated aspects of a gentleman's clothing, from his chic Borsalino hats to his glossy handmade shoes. He was willing to spend money on every item that made life agreeable.

On the other hand, I never understood my mother's attitudes to her clothes. She was always very well dressed by first-rate dressmakers and in Signor Grandi's smashing tailleurs, for which she had the ideal figure. Her *modista* (in those days, ladies always wore hats and traveled with at least one leather hatbox) was a genius at making her hats, which required several fittings and were extremely becoming to the beautiful woman my mother remained all her life. Her shoes were also made to order, but she would not spend money on silk stockings however much her friends would tell her that her lisle stockings spoiled the effect she was anxious to create. Considering the time, effort, and money my mother spent on her outfits, her claim that silk stockings wore out too quickly with runs made little sense. Especially since any Italian city had numerous women who did nothing but pull up runs and mend silk stockings (these unfortunate women could be seen sitting in the windows of some little shop, ruining their eyesight in these inevitably dimly lit places, and all for a very few pennies). Like my mother, I wore fine, flesh-colored lisle hose, with black clocks down the sides. (In those pre-nylon plain stocking days, black clocks were not considered recherché and slightly wicked as they are nowadays, but an innocuous part of any kind of better stocking.) I was a well-dressed girl for whom my mother's expensive dressmaker made "good" dresses from costly silks. I will never forget my first real party dress of madonna-blue taffeta, with a most becoming very large beige collar of real Venice lace. As a novelty, the dress had a Norfolk belt, that is, the back of the dress was belted, leaving the front plain, better to show off the lace collar. I also recollect that an elegant German bachelor, on a visit to Milan, said in my hearing that the dress was much too unsophis-

ticated for a German Consul's daughter, who "needed awakening," a remark that so angered my father that he shut up like
a clam. My mother, equally angry with the German, also never
spoke to him again. What still puzzles me is why my mother,
wearing an expensive hat and expensive clothes, would rather
risk unexpected rain than take a taxi home.

To get back to my father's spoiled-child attitude—he was a
charming, affable man when well, and an absolute monster when
ill, fussy, balking at all doctors' prescriptions—in short, an
impossible patient. In those days, and especially if a trip to the
nearest private hospital was not worthwhile, one hired nurses to
look after the patient at home. The sisters of one order were the
best nurses; among them, the most famous was an elderly and
somewhat frail-looking nun, whom my mother hired when she
could not cope any longer with my sick father's antics. The old
nun had very little trouble in calming down my tempestuous
father. How? My mother told me that whenever my father
started being impossible, the old nun would get down on her
knees and start praying loudly to the Lord for his salvation. This
went on for a day, and since the nun could pray longer and
louder than my father could fuss, she won out. My mother said
that when he realized that he would invariably lose in what
amounted to a shouting match, my father gave up his shenanigans and became putty in sister's hands. She added, with the
expression of the cat who has swallowed the canary, that ever
after, when my father was sick in bed, he would behave immediately at the mere mention of the possibility of the sister-nurse's
return.

Some of our Milan friends were Jews. My parents' attitude
about Jews was that some people were Jewish, others Germans,
or Italians, Protestants, Catholics, homosexuals, nym-
phomaniacs, atheists, conservatives, liberals, socialists, and so
forth. Like all the people we knew, we liked people or did not
like them; everything else was their own private business. Until
Hitler, I never even knew anti-Semitism to exist, and I don't
think that my parents ever thought of it either. Years later, my

father told me that what it meant to be Jewish became a reality
to him when he saw that benches in a Berlin park had a big sign
forbidding Jews to sit on them! But at the time about which I
am writing, the Hitler regime was still in the future, though, no
doubt, all of its horrors were festering already under covers.
Meantime, that pleasant, orderly life of ours went on.

The German Consulate became more and more stabilized as
time went on. A new General Consul turned up, whom we saw
a good deal of, though thinking back, the GK *(Generalkonsul)*
must have handicapped my father quite a good deal. The situation was indeed an anomalous one: here was my father, very well
known by all Italians and on friendly terms with the Italian
government authorities, the journalists, and other molders of
public opinion, and on the other side, the very correct but stiff
German professional diplomat who was indeed boss, but who
could not have functioned at all without my father's connections.
My mother created difficulties in that ambiguous situation, because the GK's wife had been a secretary before her marriage,
and therefore was looked down on by my mother. The GK's wife
was a charming, kind, and diplomatic creature who was immensely popular with anybody who met her. But my mother also
knew when she was beaten, and thus she managed to keep on
polite terms with the lady.

Both the GK and his wife were given to nature, which as-
tounded the German colony. Once, they invited us to spend a
day on the shore of Lake Maggiore, where they were camping
every weekend. My mother was bored sitting on a blanket on
the shore, but my father and I had a happy day cavorting in the
gently lapping, tepid waters of the lake. We all did enjoy the
frankfurters our hosts roasted on sticks over an open fire, for
which my father and I had gathered driftwood. The GK told us
that he kept meals deliberately as simple as possible, adding
with quiet pride that we could also have some bread and cheese,
as well as some fruit. What the natives of Lake Maggiore
thought of a high German official, unshaved and unwashed, and

dressed in dilapidated shorts, and of his equally dégagé lady, we did not know, mercifully.

Despite our knowing so many Germans in Milan, my mother remained Italian in her attitudes and habits. She was haughty with her new, posh dressmaker and with the various women who came to the house with her made-to-measure intimate garments. On the other hand, she was very friendly with the owner of a small notions shop opposite our house. The Signorina Stoppa owned a much-loved parrot. This talented bird could whistle the official Fascist song, "Giovinezza," so well that he attracted any number of customers to the shop, where he was kept in a cage just by the front door or, when the weather permitted, outside of the door in the street. Alas, *sic transit gloria mundi.* After the fall of Fascism, when Mussolini had been hung by his feet in one of Milan's popular squares, the Stoppa parrot, still whistling lustily "Giovinezza," had to be kept inside the owner's apartment since the song did sit very badly with the new post-Fascist regime.

My mother was also very fond of the two Anghileri sisters, who lived in a dark old apartment house on a narrow street opposite the Brera Palace, which houses one of the world's major art galleries. Both sisters were small, dark-haired middle-aged ladies who dressed quietly but well and who felt totally secure in everything they thought and did, suffering from neither inferiority nor superiority complexes.

Maria, the older woman, was quiet and very soft spoken. Annetta, the younger of the two, had a fiery, adventurous temperament, which would have served her well in a less traditional society than the one she lived in. Both sisters were unmarried. Why Maria had not married, I do not know since she was a very private soul, but Annetta's story was a tragic and typically Milanese one of the period. It appears that in her early twenties, the girl had become engaged to a doctor from Sicily. The wedding date had been set, the church reserved, and the invitations had gone out when the widowed Signora Anghileri, Annetta's mother, called off the whole marriage. Three days before the day, the Signora Anghileri had found out that Annetta's fiancé had had an affair in Sicily with a woman who had borne him a son. The affair had long since been over, and the illegitimate son and his mother had been handsomely provided for by Annetta's fiancé. But Annetta's mother, like almost all Milanese, hated southern Italians with a passion, so that she thought nothing of exposing her young daughter to ridicule rather than having her wed the Sicilian, whose sins were very much in the past. Annetta acted like the dutiful Italian daughter she was. She never spoke of the humiliation her mother had inflicted on her, and never complained. The old Signora Anghileri was still alive when I first knew Annetta; until her dying day, she ruled her family in a soft-spoken, affable iron way that frightened even my mother.

The flat in which the sisters Anghileri lived was in an eighteenth-century house that had been cut up into about two dozen apartments. To get there, one went up a dark staircase until, on the fourth floor, a dark landing was reached where a balcony hung over a large covered hall. On the always tightly locked balcony door was the Anghileri's nameplate. You rang their bell, the balcony door opened by remote control, and you walked the length of the balcony to their front door where somebody was waiting for you. There were two other apartments on the landing, with the customary apartment front doors, but the Anghileri's was the only one that reminded me of a hideaway that ensured safety to its occupiers.

Once inside the apartment, one was charmed to see what ingenuity and money could do with an old-fashioned place. True, the bathroom was off the front hall, but it had every modern appliance, including a hot water heater that dispensed boiling water at all times. The *salotto* and the adjoining dining room were off the passage that started at the front hall. Their furniture was richly carved and the furnishings covered with fine tapestries. A very large and very expensive television set, bought as soon as TV sets were available in Italy, had been placed in front of the dining table. At the end of the passage and flanked by the sisters' bedrooms was all that one could ask from a modern kitchen. I never saw Annetta's bedroom, but Maria's room, where guests were put up, was furnished like a drawing room, with a couch made up into a bed every night. When guests occupied Maria's bedroom, she slept on the couch in the *salotto.*

A large number of small objects were displayed throughout the house. Little silver boxes, large and small photographs in polished silver frames, enameled boxes, bud vases, and the like occupied all available space on the tables in every room. The larger or more precious knickknacks sat each on its own embroidered white doily, which in turn brought attention to all the highly polished wood surfaces and the stern neatness of the apartment.

The Anghileri sisters were so much a part of our lives that I cannot describe their lives chronologically from when I first knew them as a young girl. Both sisters had jobs that must have paid well, judging from the constant improvements to their apartment and their very pleasant way of living. Maria was a bookkeeper to a major manufacturer of church textiles, a firm that dealt only with high-echelon clerics. The most interesting of Annetta's many jobs was that of being the accountant for Modugno, at that time Italy's most famous pop singer. She used to tell us of the disorderly lives of the singer and his family, making it entirely credible that she must have been invaluable to her employers. Maria kept house and was cook when Demetria, their maid, could not work. Like so many Milanese ladies, she used to rush home from work at lunchtime, get the food on the table, eat it, and then rush back to her job, her lunch hours being twelve to two.

Italian-style, we ate our main meal in the middle of the day. Demetria was very good at cooking the saffron-scented yellow Risotto alla Milanese; this most famous of all Italian dishes requires patience to make. The dish is cooked very slowly and the liquid necessary to cook the rice is added in as small a dose as possible, since all the liquid must be absorbed before any more is added to the simmering rice. The result is a very creamy rice, each grain meltingly tender yet separate from its neighbor. A good risotto has to be eaten as soon as it is ready or it will be mushy. I remember Annetta Anghileri telling me of a certain restaurant in Milan where the risotto was served in heated wooden bowls to keep it warm without overcooking it to a mush.

For risotto, it is important to use the right kind among the many kinds of rice. In Italy, arborio rice will give the best results; the long-grain rice of the Orient, converted or not, will not make a good risotto, though it will make the best pilafs. Though rice is not nearly as nutritious as wheat, it is the staple starch of many countries, including China, Africa, Persia, India, and Turkey. And all these nations cook their own kinds of rice in their own ways.

Yellow Risotto alla Milanese is by no means the only way rice is cooked in Italy. Served in *bianco,* white rice is made plain with butter and grated Parmesan cheese, or lightly sauced with mushrooms and other vegetables, but never with a heavy tomato sauce that would overwhelm the rice's delicate flavor. White rice can also form the shell of a timbale, stuffed with a delicious savory mixture of meats, or it can be served with a white sauce rich with mozzarella cheese.

In northern Italy, where the rice is grown under water in the fat and fertile valley of the Po River, dogs are fed with leftover rice husks; "dog rice" the produce is called, and it is sold in ten-kilogram bags in neighborhood supermarkets. (In the pasta-eating regions of Italy, such as Tuscany, the neighborhood supermarkets sell "dog pasta" in similar ten-kilogram bags. Many years later, when I bought some for the large dog we had in Italy, the supermarket owner told me to try it myself, adding that during World War II most Italians would have been glad to eat dog pasta themselves. Naturally, I boiled some of the brown pasta, made from whole-wheat cullings, and it tasted good, especially when mixed with the *fondo di padella,* the butter or oil and odds and ends of food that remain in the frying pan after cooking.)

By the way, the word ending *-otto,* as in risotto, means "big" in Italian. Thus a risotto is a big dish, served by itself as a first course. In Italy, too, rice is always the first course, and never an accompaniment to meat or fish, as in France. The only exception to this iron rule is Ossobuco alla Milanese, a tasty dish of calf's shanks, accompanied by a yellow risotto.

Thinking of rice, I remembered a charming, though not entirely truthful, little poem I discovered years ago in a lovely book called *Food* written by A. L. Simon in the "Pleasures of Life" series (Burke Publishing Co., London, 1949):

How nice
Is rice!

How gentle and how very free from vice
Are those whose fodder is mainly Rice!

Rice! Rice!
Really it doesn't want thinking of twice:
The gambler would quickly abandon his dice,
The criminal classes be quiet as mice
If carefully fed upon nothing but Rice.

Yes: Rice! Rice!
Beautiful Rice!
All the wrong in the world would be right in a trice
If everyone fed upon nothing but Rice.

One of the reasons why I am fond of this poem is that the (wisely) anonymous author disregards the fact that not all rice-eating people are quiet as mice, which, by the way, are not at all quiet animals. Greeks, Turks, Indians, and Chinese—rice eaters all—may be free from vice depending on how you look upon vice, but they are rather ruthless in their approach to many aspects of life.

Truffled Risotto alla Milanese . . . how I long for it, this truffled delight. The truffles were sold in the fall in a little gallery on Milan's large Piazza del Duomo. I shall never forget the powerful truffle aroma that one smelled several streets away. It was easy to believe that the truffle men, who traveled long distances to sell their produce in Milan for very good prices, did so in the solitary comfort of their train compartments. The odor of the truffles was intolerable for anybody not in the truffle business, so much so that women were advised to pack fresh truffles if they wanted to be left alone during a train trip.

To come back to meals at the Anghileris: For midday dinner a meat dish appeared on the table as a matter of course. Breaded veal cutlets and quickly sautéed thick slices of veal or beef served with a green salad or a seasonal vegetable followed as the main course. For dessert we ate fresh fruit or a slice of Demetria's fabulous fruitcake. We finished off the meal with a little cup of espresso that was served at the table rather than in the *salotto*.

Our evening meals were also typically Italian. Maria always prepared the soup for *la cena* since Demetria had gone home to her husband and children. Maria's soups were excellent, light yet substantial, a fine start for a meal that was traditionally on the small and light side. It always included a creamy cheese. I shall never forget what Maria and Annetta told me about Mascarpone, that fresh Italian cream cheese that has now become popular in New York. I never have eaten Mascarpone here in America because I know that to be perfect it must be as fresh as can be, made preferably only the day before it is to be consumed, and how can it be that in New York? Mascarpone was originally a product of Lombardy; to be perfect, it should be made in small quantities by a small producer. Maria had close relations with one such maker whose Mascarpone was unforgettably delicious.

The sisters' way of decorous living was never more pronounced than in their way of serving anything, be it a glass of water, a cup of tea, or a single aspirin, on a tray lined with a heavily embroidered white doily. When I once asked who washed and ironed the doilies when Demetria was absent, both sisters admitted, with a touch of surprise, that they did. This in turn surprised me, because my mother would never have dreamt of doing such a thing.

Like most Milanese, the Anghileris must have been very savvy with their money to keep up their way of living. As the years went on, their apartment sported more and more improvements; more small objects crowded the sidetables and shelves, and more expensive gadgets turned up in their kitchen. How all this was paid for, I never knew, since money was never discussed. Since the subject of money was strictly taboo at our own home, I never wondered about the Anghileris' quiet prosperity. (Living in Italy, one took it for granted that everybody was out for himself, and never mind how.) Thus, it seemed absolutely normal to me that Annetta had her own car long before other ladies like her became sufficiently independent to have one. Her car and its successor were tiny Fiats, built for the comfort of only their driver. Annetta was a very good, energetic one, and very likely the thwarted passion of her nature found some release in her fast and furious driving. Distances held no terror for her. My husband, who stayed with the Anghileris several times without me, remembers with fear to this day Annetta's long Sunday drives to distant places. But he agrees with me that the two Anghileri sisters were the most hospitable souls in this world, at least as far as we were concerned.

3. BERLIN

*M*y parents' interest in my education was quite genuine, provided it was not too expensive or inconvenient, and would get me out of the house as well. In their honor, I must say that marriage for me later on never entered their heads, nor did it mine.

It had always been taken for granted that I would support myself in the career that seemed to suit me best: journalism. Since I was adventurous and intelligent, as well as curious and good at languages, the choice was obvious. As far as we all knew, one did not need any training beyond shorthand, typing, and a smattering of languages to be a journalist; one learned on the job. Which I did, later on. But meantime, I had to be educated.

Both my parents, though very liberal with their views, felt that the stiff-necked, old-fashioned Prussian way with the young developed character. Thus they consulted with some very conservative Germans, including the Lutheran minister, who recommended a *pensionnat* for girls run by a lady called Thusnelda Gess in Wernigerode, a picturesque little old resort town. Wernigerode lies in the Harz Mountains, one of Germany's loveliest regions, which today belongs to East Germany.

I still have the catalogue of the establishment. It says that a limited number of young girls between the ages of twelve and twenty will be accepted (with the exclusion of Jewesses), who will be taught religion, German grammar and literature, French and English conversation, grammar, and literature, world history, history of art, social history, geography, bookkeeping, hygiene, civics, needlework, deportment, and gymnastics. Italian, music, drawing, and painting. Dancing, typing, and shorthand were not included in the curriculum, but could be obtained. Besides, the girls were expected to do the chores of the daughter of the house, and they would be also instructed in cooking, baking, housework, sewing, knitting, and the mending of household linens. The catalogue also specified that medical care, laundry, baths, service, and the use of the piano would be charged for separately, and that each student had to bring her own horsehair mattress unless she chose to sleep on the springs. In this case, she would have to bring along a spring cover, besides bed linens, bedspread, a bedroom rug, towels, napkins, and a complete set of silver. Then the catalogue goes on to extol the virtues of Fraulein Gess's education, which strengthened body and mind, as testified to in a series of admiring remarks from parents of the aristocracy, who apparently felt that Thusnelda was as great a woman as her namesake, the wife of Arminius, the famous general of the Cherusci who defended Varus and his legions. Thusnelda behaved extremely nobly when she fell into the hands of the Romans. One parent even said so.

The *pensionnat*, described to my parents as throbbing with girls and any number of teachers to instruct them, actually had only one pupil besides myself, a large lump descended from the Prussian aristocracy. Since her father was a bona fide count, she was immensely dear to Thusnelda. Irmgard constantly received from home large parcels of substantial food like butter, *Wurst*, bread, preserves, and the like, since Thusnelda was too poor to feed us properly. What impressed me about this bovine daughter of Prussia's landed gentry, who did not believe in sharing her goodies, was that, when fishing in the ancestral trout stream, she would keep her best worms in her mouth rather than in a container. She also showed me how to accomplish this unusual feat, puffing up her cheeks. I was very impressed with it, all the more since I'd never seen it duplicated by anyone else.

Thusnelda had an underpaid assistant who looked rather like herself. Both women were ancient and creased, not only in their faces, but also in the indefinite black garments they wore. Each head of gray hair was tied in a knob on the top, rather insecurely I thought, looking at Thusnelda lecturing us two girls on the duties of a German woman. Unfortunately, she was not as specific on the subject as she might have been. In spite of her air of command, she was incapable of being specific about anything. Instead of instructing us in the running of a household, Thusnelda spoke of her own past as the mistress of one. After one lesson, I was excused from French since I knew more of the language than Thusnelda's assistant. The same happened with German literature; Thusnelda was shocked at the number and kinds of books I had read. However, I was allowed to wallow to my heart's content in German romantic and lyrical poetry. My lifelong love for German romantic and lyrical poetry was formed during the two or three months I spent in the Tochler *pensionnat*.

Apart from the faulty instruction, things did not go too well almost from the beginning. From a number of my letters home which have survived the vicissitudes of my life, I see that I was very homesick, but determined to be the model of hard work, probity, and studiousness that was expected of me by both my parents and Thusnelda. My appearance did not meet with Thusnelda's approval. I was made to wear my long hair in two coils over the ears, a fashion suited for *Deutsche Mädchen*, so I was told. To behave like a proper German girl was an endlessly repeated litany, which included being silent when Thusnelda and her assistant lashed out at the Weimar Republic and its leaders. This naturally upset me very much, having lived in very liberal surroundings, where the current leadership of Germany was regarded as bliss compared to that of the unlamented kaiser of World War I days.

With the charitable hindsight of my years, I think that Thusnelda simply could not cope any longer with the residues of the German inflation and the lost war. The great German inflation was about to be settled with the introduction of a totally new German currency, the deutsche reichsmark. I must have been in Wernigerode during the very last days of the inflation debacle when a letter abroad cost 30 million marks and when all prices were rising so fast into the upper millions that one went shopping as early in the morning as possible, to buy life's necessities at yesterday's prices before they were upped by millions later in the day. This incredible inflation cannot be understood by anyone who did not live through it. It is, among others, one of the reasons for Hitler's rise. Avoiding a big inflation and its consequences accounts for German politics to this day, as any German politician knows very well.

I gather that my parents paid for me in Italian *lire;* foreign currencies were the only money worth having in inflationary Germany. I was given pocket money in foreign currencies, though never enough to pay for my expenses. (In one of my letters I told my parents that fixing a pair of heels cost 100,000 million marks!) I was constantly begging for a clothes brush, soap, doe woolen gloves, mending yarn, and similar small-time necessities. Above all, there were the food parcels sent to me largely by my socialist-liberal father, who must have had some qualms at having me live among the blackest of German reactionaries. In truth, I was always hungry. Thusnelda was no longer able or willing to run her institution properly. The food was as scanty as it was simple. For instance, each of us had one pancake and some green salad one night, another night we had potatoes in their skins and a small herring. What I resented was that Thusnelda and her assistant were served some extra food at the same time, such as meat and vegetables, and that the two women drank real coffee, made with real coffee beans, while Irmgard and I had to drink some horrible vegetable mixture that passed as coffee *Ersatz*. The food parcels from home by no means contained the usual goodies sent to kids in boarding school. The spaghetti, rice, barley, olive oil, tomato paste, and canned vegetables were basic fare, considered as part of my tuition and board expenses.

My parents never came to Wernigerode, but my father sent one of his lady friends from Berlin to see what was really the matter. I still have her letter describing the morass she found. Addressed to my mother, this celestial vision, as I described her in one of my letters, Fräulein Neumann, related how she was invited for supper (bread and margarine, radishes, and home-fried potatoes) after being quizzed at length about her origin, education, earnings, jobs, and personal attachments. My father and mother were also investigated at length at the same time, since he was not an aristocrat and especially since my mother, an Italian child, could have been of undesirable ancestry. After supper, for which Thusnelda had dressed up in her best antiquated, dusty black silk dress, with a parure of jet stones, I was sent out of the room and the complaints about me cascaded forth like water over a broken dam. I was illiterate, sassy, and too stupid to be educated properly. Referring to a letter from my father in which he said that he was a German civil servant on a fixed salary and not a robber baron able to send more and more money, it appeared that the low-watt electric bulb in my room used enough electricity to swallow all my school fees, to quote just one incident.

Fräulein Neumann thought that there was no future in my staying in Wernigerode since I could learn to play the piano, shorthand, and typing anywhere in Germany. She felt that my parents were paying for my having become the chief shopper and money changer for Thusnelda. This meant that every day I was standing in line to buy potatoes and making the rounds of all the town's banks and money changers to find the best exchange rates for the mysterious dollars, crowns, and francs which Thusnelda had gotten from heaven-knows-where. I was happy to do these chores as this got me out of my stifling surroundings, but on the other hand, why did my parents pay for it?

After Fräulein Neumann's departure, things got worse. I was given a postcard to mail to my parents (Thusnelda knew full well that I would read it), in which they were accused of being avaricious.

I traveled to Berlin with my father, who had some business at the *Auswärtiges Amt,* the German Foreign Office. In Berlin, my father registered me in the Lettehaus, a rather classy vocational school with an excellent reputation. The Lettehaus offered numerous practical and secretarial courses originated in the days when the Germans, or some of them, awakened to self-improvement, vegetarianism, fresh air, and cold water. I was put under the vague tutelage of an old couple who had helped my father with photographs when he published illustrated books in Rome a long time ago. All I remember of the couple is that Frau Schwartz had a tall, commanding figure and lots of loosely pinned-up white hair. Frau Schwartz found me a room in a quiet, treelined street near the Lettehaus, which overlooked a square planted with linden trees and big, ancient, gnarled lilacs. Both the apartment house in which I was to live and the Lettehaus where I was to learn were large, ornate, antiquated buildings that dated back to the nineties. The apartment in which I was renting a room occupied the whole of the third floor. The establishment called itself a *pension* in the hope that the word would attract some other people besides myself. The place was run by the aristocratic widow of an army officer, who was constantly bemoaning her present diminished status—due to the lost war (World War I) and the following inflation, or so she said. Her apartment was so very different from anything I had ever seen in a flat that I wrote down all of its furnishings to remember them properly. My description has now emerged in a mess of family papers; I mention this just in case you wonder why I remember Frau von Stein's *pension* so well.

Frau von Stein was old and extremely poor. Her husband, dead some forty years, had been an officer of the Imperial Guard. Apparently he had become embroiled in some shady dealings with gambling debts and unpaid moneylenders. Such things were not tolerated in the Prussian army. He had been forced to turn in his resignation. This was the end of him—a young man of the aristocracy who had been reared to be an officer and nothing else. He shot himself, which was the right thing to do according to the mores of his class and his time, and a gesture that redeemed him in the eyes of his wife and his family. The alternative would have been to emigrate to America, and this he could not face.

The apartment itself was typical of Berlin. A number of rooms opened from a passage that ended in a "Berliner Zimmer," a windowless room that served as a living room and connected the front of the house with the back. The one bathroom in the flat was at the back of the house, and in order to go there you had to cross the living room.

The apartment's front part included two salons, separated by a sliding door. These dark rooms were curtained twice, once in white muslin and once in dark red and gold velour, with hand-embroidered window curtains to boot. Today, I would describe the rooms as Victorian upper class, with the usual complement of big and little plush-covered sofas and chairs, small tables laden with silver-framed signed photographs and bric-a-brac, darkly papered walls hung closely with heavily framed ancestral portraits, nature scenes, still lives, and romantic pictures of lads and lassies in costume against a backdrop of the Alps or a medieval market square. The furniture was massive, with Gothic overtones, and obviously it had once been good and expensive or it would not have lasted for some fifty years. It was also beautifully polished with beeswax; I remember asking why the furniture smelled like honey. Frau von Stein polished it herself every day. The salons were not in daily use, and the curtains were drawn to prevent whatever little light could get through in the first place from fading the upholstery and the wallpaper. But on Sundays and Thursdays the salons were opened. On Sundays we sat in one of them after our midday dinner, and on Thursdays Frau von Stein had her *jour* when she received her friends between four and seven.

Apart from the salons, five or six rooms must have opened from the dark, narrow passage. One was the music room, containing nothing but a battle-scarred old grand, a piano bench, a few straight chairs, and a little table. The grand was draped with a Spanish embroidered shawl, a dark red one, which had to be folded each time the grand was opened for playing. On it stood an assembly of little busts of famous composers, which also had to be put away before playing. The pictures on the walls were those Germans admired about music and musicians: Beethoven pacing, hand to cheek, in a storm; the child prodigy Mozart playing to a rococo group of princes and their ladies; and a modern one that must have swept Germany since one saw it everywhere. It represented a group of people sitting on chairs in a darkened concert hall and listening to music with various rapt expressions, and obviously groaning and moaning as they wallowed in the music; I always thought it particularly repulsive. One other room served as a classroom. One wall was largely covered with a map of Imperial Germany, topped with a group portrait of the kaiser and his family. On a big shelf stood an old edition of the *Grosse Brockhaus,* a German encyclopedia, and Brehm's *Tierleben,* an encyclopedia of animal life. The other books were the German Bartlett, called *Geflügelte Werke,* and the standard editions of the German poets, from Walther von der Vogelweide through Lessing, Kleist, Schiller, Goethe, and Platen to Mörike and Fontane. Also included were the novels on which every German child is brought up—Dehn's *Der Kampf um Rom,* Scheffel's *Ekkehard,* the novels of Stifter and Storm, and of course, the works of Wilhelm Busch, one of the greatest satiric writers and draftsmen who ever lived, whose rhymes are German household words.

Frau von Stein's room was at the front, but I never saw the inside of it. My bedroom was at the back, at the other side of the dining room, and it overlooked a dark court. The furnishings were Spartan. The bed was a small iron cot; the wardrobe, tables, and chairs plain pine; the ewer, basin, and pail on the washstand and the *pot de chambre* under the bed were all unadorned coarse white china. The bathroom, too, did not invite sybaritic living. It must have dated back to Bismarck's time and the only somewhat modern appliance was a gas water heater. Here I took my weekly bath, for which I was charged separately.

Life centered in the Berliner Zimmer. This was a far more utilitarian room than the salons. The furniture, Biedermeier style, was plain and charming, but to eyes used to the excrescences of Imperial Germany, the very plainness offended and hence the relegation to the Berliner Zimmer. A large round table stood in the middle, illuminated by a hanging lamp that could be pulled up or down. The table was covered with an embroidered cloth that reached to the ground; there was a cloth for weekdays and another for Sunday. The lampshade, too, was embroidered. The room was large and dark, and the pictures did nothing to light it up. It was dominated by a life-size oil portrait of the late Baron von Stein, a handsome and weak-looking young man, mustached like his imperial chief, in the full uniform of the Imperial Guards. The other pictures were genre scenes from the Bavarian Alps and the North Sea—village maidens, fishermen, and so forth; a reproduction of the Last Supper; one of Böcklin's Isle of the Dead and one of Menzel's Frederick the Great. There was also a cluster of enlarged photographs of the funeral of the Empress Auguste Viktoria on April 11, 1921, in Potsdam, which I imagine was the last event to gather in the whole of imperial society; the women were all veiled in black crepe, the men in full uniform and decoration. Frau von Stein had been present, and she often spoke with great feeling of the sorrow they all felt because they knew that "things would never be the same again."

Frau von Stein was straight, tall, and thin. She dressed, Gibson girl fashion, in dark suits with long jackets over white blouses with frilly jabots. On her Adam's apple she wore a large regimental brooch, which moved up and down as she spoke. Her clothes were old and shabby, though extremely neat. Her face was large and white, with very light blue eyes, a pale fleshy nose, and a tight-lipped mouth. Her hair had gone yellow, and she put it up in a kind of bird's nest. Her manner was quiet, as was her voice, and she only betrayed her emotions by folding her hands so tightly that the knuckles became white. Altogether she gave an antique and rusty impression, resembling an ancient locomotive. She was constantly on the move, keeping house, straightening things, and wheezing as she did so. Whenever she sat down for a few moments, a piece of mending appeared in her hands, or else she knitted socks for her son. She sighed often, and deeply, and turned her eyes to heaven. The only time she became animated was when she told of her life as a young wife in Potsdam, where her husband had been stationed. Apparently he was well regarded at Court because of his family connections— he came from a long line of Prussian Guard officers—and for him, too, the sun rose and set with the emperor and his family. Herr and Frau von Stein, even then, had not been well-off. He was a third son from a small entailed estate in Pomerania, and she the daughter of a retired major who had barely managed to scrape up her dowry when she married the dashing officer. They did not belong to the glittering aristocracy of the East Prussian Junkers and other big military landowners and the great names that turned up constantly in the politics of Imperial Germany. The von Steins were, so to speak, the backbone of the Germany of the kaisers, rural gentry who lived and died according to an extremely rigid and even more limited code, where the first question asked about a new person or a new idea was, *"Ist er"* or *"es standesgemäss"*—does he or it conform to what's expected of our class? They were the members of the Conservatives, the German National Party, the leaders of the Stahlhelm and other groups of World War I officers and men. Like Thusnelda, they hated the Weimar Republic.

I imagine that Frau von Stein liked me because I was so very different from the young girls of her circle. She loved the theater, and took me to see the dramas of Schiller and Kleist, as well as a suitable operetta, such as the *Merry Widow.* Invariably, we went to matinees because they were much cheaper; afterward, we would go, as a treat, to a *Konditorei,* where we consumed a cup of coffee and one piece of cake each, all that Frau von Stein could afford. As Frau von Stein once admitted to me, she liked me because I had *tenue,* that is, a stiff upper lip. "Having *tenue"* was a sure sign of proper behavior, just as saying of a man that *"er jeut,"* he gambles, was the unspeakable opposite. Many years after Frau von Stein used these French expressions, it occurred to me that the spirit of Frederick the Great, who preferred French to German, was still alive in Germany's most old-fashioned circles.

Sometimes, on a Sunday afternoon, Frau von Stein invited me to have coffee with her. In her dining room the table was set with an embroidered cloth and lovely old Meissen china. I remember it especially because of the washing-up ritual of the coffee things. The china was too fine to be entrusted to the old maid in the kitchen, so, on another table, in the corner of the dining room, a cloth was spread and two basins put on it. One was filled with hot water and the other with cold water. Frau von Stein washed the cups right then and there with a soft cloth and soap; I was so surprised that, for once, I was silent.

Frau von Stein was worried about my deportment, or rather, the lack of it. Since the Lettehaus did not bother about deportment, she took it upon herself to teach me how to enter a room, how to sit down and how to get up, how to curtsy, and how to converse with different people. Frau von Stein took their part, being in turn a royal highness, a count and his countess, a high civil servant, or a tradesman who had become rich and was about to worm his way into society. I also remember Frau von Stein advising me on my personal habits. "Electricity," she said, "is expensive, and you must learn to undress in the darkness. Once a week, of course, you should take a whole bath, but during the week it is essential to wash your feet every night. Of course," she went on, looking at me sternly, "I do hope that you wash your face, ears, and neck every morning, and your whole body every other day."

Though my greatest interest was Frau von Stein and her life, I was conscious of being a Lettehaus student. I took typing and shorthand lessons every day, making good progress. But how I wish I had paid more attention to my French and English lessons, and had not given up on the piano because I could not stand the teacher, a high-bosomed lady with a perpetual sniffle. And I wish especially I had been more interested in sewing instruction, so that, all my life, I would not cringe at the sight of a sewing machine. All in all, I was not made to work, possibly because the Lettehaus was not geared to girls as young as myself. Apart from having to be dead punctual for meals, I do not remember anything about supervision.

As I am writing this, I have in front of me a little heart-shaped autograph book that opens up in an accordion fold. The cover shows the black silhouette (silhouettes were in fashion then) of a hoop-skirted lady holding a heart in each hand, with the German inscription *"oh wonnevolle Jugendzeit"* (oh, delightful time of youth). Inside, the pages are filled with rhymed exhortations to thrift, work, prudence, modesty, and sunniness in adversity. My friends' hands wrote these sentiments; all young German girls at the time owned such a memory book. In the little book I also put down my judgments on some of my Lettehaus companions. Here they are: Nina Ottens, small, blond, vivacious, and intelligent. A Russian who was different from the way she appeared. Lisa Ehms, egotistical, stupid, and greedy. Hanna Samself, whom I did not find sympathetic, small, engaged, and looking everywhere for "tender affairs." Marga Frohling, a Balt: small, reliable; Kaethe Kapernick, straight from a little village, was horrendously stupid. Hertha Huhn, made for sports, was a show-off who at times could be very nice. I did not at all like Erika Doeffel, a friend of Huhn's. Marion Drescher, almost always likable, was intelligent, serious, but very funny at times. Elli Hennig, extremely stupid and sometimes described as the innocent from the countryside, was constantly teased, whereas Lore Wohlin could at times be quite nice.

Looking back on my first long stay in Berlin, alone and free to come and go as I liked, I am now surprised that I did not know anything of Berlin's *mauvais monde*. I was rather highbrow in all my tastes and especially fond of music, above all the opera. My mother once, in her last years, showed me a letter of mine in which I bragged of the thirty-five times I had been to the opera in the six months or so I spent in Berlin and listed the celebrities whom I had heard in concerts. They included Nikisch, Toscanini, and Furtwängler. My literary tastes were equally highbrow; I preferred Voltaire to Romain Rolland and doted also on Egyptian and Medieval art, and on the Renaissance.

At this time I got to know my Berlin relatives quite well. My father's only sister, Clara, had married one of the pillars of Berlin's social-democratic party as well as of all Germany's trade unions. Both Tante Clara and Onkel Paul remained staunch socialists all of their lives, as did their two daughters, Kaethe and Hilde, each older than myself. My Uncle Paul owned and ran a tobacco shop in the *Gewerkschaftshaus*, the headquarters of German unionism, a many-gabled red brick building that overlooked one of Berlin's multiple canals. My aunt worked as a social worker in a municipal welfare agency, and devoted what little free time she had to the cause of trade unionism. Mercifully, Tante Clara and Onkel Paul were dead before Germany lost World War II and Hitler annihilated everyone in the whole socialist and democratic political German movement, but they would have been equally destroyed if the Communists had managed to control Germany. The two daughters were also dedicated to the welfare of the masses. Kaethe, the older girl, had become a counselor in Germany's great network of social agencies, while Hilde, the younger girl, had made nursing her profession. My father liked his relatives, though he kept them at a certain distance. I don't think that my mother cared for her vivacious and loquacious sister-in-law. In any event, my relatives were political people whose world I considered hemmed in by local politics, which I did not think as interesting as global affairs.

Their apartment's front rooms looked out on the spacious road along one of the city's canals, in one of the better working-class districts of Berlin, which now lies behind the Iron Curtain in East Berlin. Totally free from luxuries, it was comfortable, and very different from our apartments in Italy. I remember my aunt coming home in the evening, full of her job, as she laid the table for supper. The meal, in the true Berlin fashion, was a cold one, consisting of black bread, butter, cold cuts, and cheese, with black sugared tea as a drink, and sometimes a bottle of beer for my uncle. *Kaltes Abendbrot,* the meal was called, translated literally as a "cold evening bread." The cold supper habit must be originally north German, since it resembles, in a minor way, the cold table of adjacent Denmark. I don't like to stuff myself at night with sausages and cold cuts of various kinds, such as *Blutwurst, Mettwurst, Teewurst,* Westphalian ham, and Rhenish ham, but I admit the cold supper has the advantage of being ready when wanted since there is no heating of leftovers and/or making soup for supper as there is in Italy and France. *Kaltes Abendbrot* has the further advantage of letting you splurge as much as you want to or can afford. It must always include some form of pickled herring (in cream, or vinegar, but always with lots of onion and black peppercorns), a choice of breads (white, rye, and black), and preferably a dish of smooth *Gänseschmalz,* a spread made from goose fat (strong north German men weep when they think of it), which is used instead of butter. As for cheeses, the more the merrier, from smelly Liptauer to mild Tilsit. Genteel homemakers will decorate their spread with parsley curls, but always whatever is to be eaten is presented on its own plate.

On holidays, festive occasions, and for distinguished visitors—my uncle and aunt knew all the socialist bigwigs and were friends with a number of them—my aunt would roast a goose, carefully saving the bird's fat. Goose fat was a delicacy, especially when used instead of butter on the numerous *Stullen,* a Berlin dialect word for sandwiches. The kitchen was also typical of Berlin. The large stove was heated by gas and topped with a chimney from which dangled saucepans and frying pans. There was a big kitchen cabinet near the sink, holding dishes in its upper part and food staples in the lower part. Cold water only came out of the tap over the sink; whenever hot water was needed for washing dishes and the like, it was heated on the stove in a large kettle. I remember the coffee mill, so different from ours at home, which was a brass tower from Turkey, whereas the German coffee mill was square, wooden, and rather ordinary, I thought. However, both at home and in Berlin, coffee was freshly ground whenever coffee was made, and as the youngest person around, and one generally useless when it came to household chores, I was inevitably delegated to grind the coffee. In Italy we drank espresso immediately after our meals, but in Germany the coffee hour was around four o'clock in the afternoon, when it was served with cakes. The habit of afternoon coffee and cake was known as *Kaffeetrinken,* which became a *schön Kaffeetrinken gehen* if one went to a *Konditorei.* The habit of afternoon coffee is still alive and well in both Germanies, where one sees large, gossiping matrons consuming coffee, mounds of whipped cream, and cakes of all sorts in the local *Konditorei.* Another habit, so very different from home, that I learned about in Germany was the "second breakfast," which happened around nine to ten o'clock in the morning, and which consisted of *Stullen* accompanied by coffee, or beer for men. The second breakfast may have been a Berlin habit, but my relatives assured me, as my aunt and any available female were spreading the *Stullen* with butter and cold cuts, that it was a necessity, since breakfast was eaten early and midday dinner late, around two o'clock.

The house in which my relatives lived had the usual *Washküche,* a laundry room in the cellar, where the laundry was boiled in big caldrons by a laundress, or *Waschfrau,* about once a month, I believe. Where the enormous amounts of laundry were dried, I don't remember that I ever knew, but I know that my aunt proudly owned a *Mangel,* a wringer that smoothed the sheets and tablecloths. It stood in a corner of the kitchen, and was pulled out whenever needed.

The wooden kitchen table was scoured daily with sand, which was stored in a large sack in another kitchen corner. Here I should mention the basic difference among American and German and Italian kitchens, which persists to this day. German and Italian kitchens are empty rooms, to be furnished like the rest of the apartment or house, since no cabinets or stove or refrigerator are furnished. In the United States, to my happy surprise, I discovered that rented kitchens were not barren spaces, but that they came furnished with cabinets, stoves, and even refrigerators, which may have been antiquated but nevertheless were usable. (The rule that immovable furnishings, such as cabinets and stoves, belonged to the landlord and movable ones to the renter made good sense to me.) I presume my aunt's kitchen was a rather simple and old-fashioned one, and that the kitchens in homes of the rich in Berlin's upper-class quarters were much more modern. But I did not know such places and, in any case, my lack of interest in the mechanics of housekeeping was total.

My Berlin relatives, who lived so differently from us, taught me that comfort is a relative matter; more importantly, I learned from them tolerance for others. I did not know it at the time, but they are really responsible for my having been able to adjust to all the new circumstances of my later life.

Until I came to America, I had been to Berlin so many times, and always for a short time only, that I find it impossible to date accurately the events that I remember best. It must have been on an early visit that I learned to love the town's surroundings, the many lakes, forests, fields, and meadows of the Mark Brandenburg, the province that surrounds Berlin. I came to know this still unspoiled rustic landscape through the *Wanderschaften,* the wanderings or excursions on foot that I went on with my cousins. These wanderings were an outcome of the youth movement of 1896 when young men and women, called *Wandervögel,* wandering birds, took to the country complete with guitars, sleeping out of doors whenever they could, and going in for ethical culture, health foods, and fresh-air living—all that was so contrary to the stuffy mores of their times. In Italy I had not been affected by the stuffiness and hypocrisy of old Germany, but I had seen enough of it to despise it wholeheartedly. At the time, the only way I could take part in my cousins' life-styles was to go wandering with them. In an old letter to my father, I find a description of such a *Fahrt* to a little town called Neuruppin. The town is situated in Mark Brandenburg, which is known to be extremely sandy. The province is a storehouse of nostalgia, and is also known for its series of lakes, which nestle in pine and birch forests. I am not nostalgic about the place, but I admit its peaceful, idyllic charm, and I can well understand the kind of gentle melancholia it inspires when one wanders through it.

My two cousins, a girl friend of theirs, and I wandered among small lakes and forests, interspersed with moors where heather and forget-me-nots flowered surprisingly side by side. We had left Berlin early on Saturday morning by train. We first visited Rheinsberg, one of Frederick the Great's little country châteaux, which impressed us with its very plain and simple furnishings. I remember that the vaguely Georgian chairs were made of light cherrywood. We admired the beautiful park along the castle's own lake, a rather vivacious sandstone garden, a pyramid erected for Prince Heinrich (the great Frederick's younger brother), and two stone sphinxes, representing Madame de Pompadour and the Empress Maria Theresa. We were tired, but we felt it our duty to look at the small, unappealing village of Kleinklersdorf, which consisted of a short row of low white-washed houses strung along the main, very dusty road. We stayed overnight at the Deutsches Hotel, decorated with many pictures of the departed kaiser, still revered by the hotel owners, where we were were given a miserable supper of hashed browns and pickled herring.

The next day we walked to the very big Stechlin Lake, enjoying a landscape of pines and heather where many birds were singing out their hearts. In an inn on the lake border, we drank some cold water mixed with raspberry juice, which was the standard soft drink of the times. A poor watery drink it was, to judge from my remarks about it. We walked in the birch and pine forest around the lake, and rested on a very high ridge above it. Finally, we got to a very humdrum and conservative little town called Fürstenberg. On this Sunday evening, the locals paraded in all their finery, and looked at our dégagé appearance with horrified curiosity. There were a lot of people around, especially many *Wandervögel*, with guitars and in short pants. (We must remember that, then, short pants and casual dressing were a sure sign that the wearers rebelled against society.) According to my notes, we went to have coffee and cake in an extremely philistine inn, where we spent a lot of time writing cynical poetry about the excursion; the four-line verses were good, scanning and rhyming properly, and dealt with Frederick the Great, his castle, and the red-nosed, drunken tour guide and his patriotic speeches.

I loved these country rambles because I did not have the obligation to be pleasant or to make sure that the trip would be a success. By the time I went to Berlin, I really was a nature freak. My mother, as I said, adored being on top of a very high mountain that could only be reached by a minimum of five hours of steady walking uphill. Walking for long hours did not faze me since I was used to it from an early age, from the time my mother took me with her to Swiss resorts where we would walk for hours up and down steep inclines.

One blissful summer I discovered the joys of rock-climbing. My mother rented an apartment in the Italian Dolomites; it was in Sankt Ulrich in Gröden, now called Ortisei in Val Gardena by the Italians, who won that part of the Austrian Tyrol after World War I. Sankt Ulrich was then no longer a part of the Tyrol, but of the province of Bolzano, named for the region's main city, Bolzano, formerly Bozen. Bozen was famous in its own right for its charming architecture, for its arcades, and for being the center of the wine and fruit trade; grapes, apples, and cherries as well as other fruits grow extremely well on the sunny hills that surround it, which are shaded by the rocky great Dolomites.

The Italians did their best to Italianize the region. At the time I was there they had not yet succeeded in converting the town and mountain village populations to their way of administering the Alto Adige, the Tyrol's new Italian name. Some of the valleys were Italian, notably the one where the world-famous resort of Cortina d'Ampezzo lies. Others, like Bozen, were completely Austrian and German speaking, and still others, like the Val Gardena, once Grödnerthal, were "Ladinos." This meant that these mountain valleys had been settled centuries ago by Roman soldiers; though their way of daily living was Germanic rather than Italian, the mountain people spoke Ladin, or Romansch, a Latin dialect that is another language. One also encounters it in a few valleys of far eastern Switzerland in the canton of Grisons, settled by the Romans at about the same time.

Thinking back, I recollect that my mother chose Sankt Ulrich because one of her better maids came from there—the pretty and stubborn but very capable Anna, who sang melancholy songs in pidgin German that I remember to this day. In any case, the place sounded wonderful, with big fir forests, Alpine pastures, and climbable mountains all around the little village. (Nowadays, Sankt Ulrich, or Ortisei, has become a busy and quite elegant summer and winter resort, along with the lesser villages in the valley.) The one hotel—today there are many— was fully booked all summer. Therefore my mother, also hoping to save some money, took an apartment in the house of the Obletter family, which consisted of father, mother, two sons, and a daughter.

Father Obletter was, like almost all the men in the town, a sculptor in wood. His were the figures of saints, naturalistically painted, which are seen in a large number of Europe's Roman Catholic churches. Wood sculpture used to be the economic backbone of the valley before tourism became popular. Not only were ecclesiastic or devotional carved wooden objects made by the wood sculptors but also secular objects. All wood carvings were dried out of doors in the summer air, so that walking around became also an exercise in judging the talents and executions of Sankt Ulrich's sculptors.

Father Obletter was a nice, outgoing man who let his wife do the worrying in the family. I don't remember much of their children, except that Frau Obletter, in a black dress and a blue apron, worried constantly over their morals. She was not wrong about the cause of her concerns, because in the dusk of the evenings, they canoodled like everyone who was not married, in the shade of the painted sacred statues and holy ornaments that gave a strange, surrealistic air to the sedate, large peasant houses of the town.

Of that first summer in Sankt Ulrich I only remember that I walked relentlessly with my mother, up and down the lesser Dolomites. I also had developed a taste and a gift for rock-climbing, which my mother could not do, since hanging on a rope on a sheer rock, a three-way abyss yawning under her, made her nervous. But rock-climbing exhilarated me and it got me in with the rock-climbing youths, male and female, of Sankt Ulrich. One of the virtues of Dolomite rock-climbing is that few of the climbs are the all-day procedures one encounters when scaling mountains covered with glaciers and ice, for which one has to be properly equipped with crampons and ice axes in addition to the ubiquitous rope. We could master one of the peaks in a few hours with our rope-soled, nonslippery shoes, some simple pieces of equipment, and, of course, a rope.

My mother liked the vast fir-tree forests and the Alpine meadows of Sankt Ulrich, and she liked the Obletter's apartment. It was simply but comfortably furnished with the solid, gaily painted peasant furniture of the Austrian Tyrol. Though we always spoke German to the Obletters, who spoke Ladin to each other, my mother and I conversed in Italian because, other than the two of us, nobody spoke that language.

Frau Obletter used to cook for us. Then, and on the many other occasions when I stayed with the Obletter family—alone, mind you—I learned to savor the simple, tasty food of the Tyrol. Frau Obletter's dumplings were spectacular. Called *Knoedel*, the German word for dumplings, they were made from stale bread, chopped into fine pieces, and held together with beaten eggs, a little flour, and a drop of water, and filled in various ways. Sometimes the fist-sized dumplings were interspersed with pieces of *Speck* (bacon), which made them into *Speckknoedel;* other times, we had *Leberknoedel,* with chopped fried liver. Sometimes they were made mostly from potatoes, which made them into *Kartoffelknoedel,* but these were never as light as those made from stale bread. Frau Obletter steamed her *Knoedel,* except when she wrapped the plain dough into a napkin and tied and boiled it to make *Serviettenknoedel.* These were always sliced and eaten with boiled meat, whereas the steamed dumplings were served with a salad. This food was so much part of Tyrolean life that there were *Knoedel*-eating competitions held at local fairs, where strong men ate as much as three dozen of what is essentially a heavy clinker. Personally, I was content with two *Knoedel,* as were most women and children. Thus, a full Tyrolean meal cooked by Frau Obletter would consist of bouillon, always made with beef, and served with a hunk of fresh bread to dip into the plain broth. Then came the meat with some kind of *Knoedel.* Dessert was one of Frau Obletter's fantastically airy strudels, filled with apples, and ground walnuts from the tree in the backyard.

Making a really good strudel dough is a great achievement since the dough must be so thin that you can read through it, but still be soft and pliable so that it can be rolled up around the filling. (This art, rarer than you think, of making a first-class strudel can only be achieved by much practice.) Frau Obletter put a clean tablecloth on the kitchen table, floured it lightly, and then fussed around with the strudel dough, pulling it into an increasingly thinner sheet with both hands held up at chest height. Finally, layer upon layer, she rolled it up over the filling, baked it in her wood oven, and saw it totally eaten at the next meal, for who on earth can resist a freshly baked, fragrant strudel?

Our meals may have been starchy, but we thrived on them, having spent so many hours in the clear mountain air that made us extremely hungry. After this first summer in Sankt Ulrich, I visited the Obletters many times by myself. (Even now, I cannot bear to call the village by its Italian name, Ortisei.) I remember especially one Christmas spent there, happy to be among my adored Dolomites once more. The snow had come early that year. Like everybody else in the valley, I knew how to ski. In those days the best skis were made out of hickory wood, and ski lifts had not yet been invented. If there was a road or a path up to where you wanted to ski, you carried your skis on your shoulders and trudged uphill. If there was no path, you put on your skis and zigzagged up to one high mountain meadow after the other, groaning and grumbling that you would have to come down eventually. There was nothing else to do if you wanted to ski. After years of modern skiing, with special boots, fiberglass skis, and other fancy equipment, I still sigh for the old-fashioned skiing of my youth.

How well I remember trudging uphill for three or four hours to a special Alpine hut on a Saturday night. My companions, all local boys and girls, and I left Sankt Ulrich after supper in the dark with the stars as our only lights. In the hut, we danced to an old-fashioned phonograph, the kind that lets out the sound through a big hearing trumpet. We skied back early on Sunday morning and arrived in town in time for the first mass at 6:00 A.M., which we attended. In Sankt Ulrich I got acquainted with the habit of its men, who spent their time leaning against the walls of the church, gossiping away like magpies, and entering only during the holiest moment of the Catholic mass, the Elevation. The parish priest and the wives of these casual churchgoers raved and ranted against such a delinquent way of going to Sunday mass, but to no avail.

During that wonderful Christmas holiday I became ill from

overeating on Frau Obletter's large, rich, and delicious cookies. Thus I made the acquaintance of the local doctor, a golden-bearded Viking of a man from Bozen. He and I liked each other sufficiently for him to take me along when he visited his patients in the outlying districts; I still have a picture of both of us walking along a snowy road, with the gray, snow-patched Dolomites in the background. He liked me better than I liked him, but I have never forgotten the words he said to me when we said a final good-bye to each other. "I will carry my burden," he said, "until Eastertime. But then I will lay my sorrows in the Holy Grave and, with the help of the Lord, start life anew."

4. ENGLAND

*N*ext, I was sent to school in England. Anglophilia was rampant in Europe at that time, and what better chance for me to perfect my English without costing my parents any school fees? I was to be an *au pair* girl at St. Mary's Hill School, and I would talk French, German, and Italian to the pupils in exchange for my board and classes. The school's address was Horsell, Woking, Surrey. In those days, Surrey and Woking were not as suburban as they are now. Small, provincial Woking was our nearest town, about half an hour's walk from the school, through some pretty countryside. Horsell, our village, consisted of a few houses scattered along a main road. The school stood in its own spacious grounds on a ridge just below the Horsell parish church with its square Norman tower. St. Mary's Hill School was housed in an extremely large Victorian-built private house, surrounded by gardens, two tennis courts, and a field where students played hockey and lacrosse. In England lacrosse is played like field hockey; the merry head bashing with the special lacrosse sticks was—and probably still is—in full flower.

The school was run and owned by the two Misses Dubochet. Gertrude, the older one and the headmistress, was a great lady with the air of utter command in any situation. Nothing ever escaped her sharp eyes, which belied her round nose and chin and her full, soft mouth. She was always "Miss Dubochet" to all and sundry, whereas Alice, her younger sister, was invariably called "Miss Alice." Miss Dubochet was still a beautiful woman who knew her charms. She was always exquisitely dressed in fine silks and splendid tweeds; her white, soft hair framed her face in soft waves, even when she wore a stylish hat. Miss Alice was on the homely side. Quite a bit taller than her sister, she was rather shapeless and dressed in rather shapeless tweeds. Miss Alice was hardly ever seen without her hat, which matched her tweeds; brown was her color.

Miss Dubochet lived at the school proper, but Miss Alice's domain was The Cottage, down the hill from St. Mary's Hill. Miss Alice, who had met me in London's Victoria Station when I arrived all by myself from Milan, took me there even before I was introduced to her sister. She showed me my bedroom under the eaves of The Cottage, which indeed was a cottage, nondescript outside, but cozy inside, with a lot of upholstered furnishings and knickknacks downstairs, where Miss Alice resided. The upstairs bedrooms, where I and two of the students slept, could not have been plainer. I do not remember anything of my trip to England, or of my first days in the school, except that it was clear to me that I was Miss Alice's responsibility in all but study matters. Miss Alice was the musical of the two sisters, and she never let one forget it, though not objectionably so. The grand piano in her living room was seldom silent during the day when her piano pupils were taking their lessons. Miss Alice had studied piano in London for a long time. Together with her genuine love for good (and I stress good) music and her accomplished teaching methods, she inspired her pupils as did no other piano teacher I have known before or since. I wish I had been one of them, but my mother had made it very clear to me that I was in England to study the language and not to take special lessons that had to paid for, since they were not included in my *au pair* deal. But I loved music and I loved hearing Miss Alice tell me about Ebenezer Trout, a famous Victorian London piano teacher. She quoted me snatches of rhymes that Victorian man had made up to remind his pupils of certain J. S. Bach pieces. Whenever I hear the Bach fugue Ebenezer wanted to impress upon his pupils, I automatically sing along these words: "Oh Ebenezer Trout, you are a funny man, you make Bach's fugues as funny as you can," and "Ebenezer Trout sat upon a tack, and he got up with a HOWL!" and from Bach's *Well-Tempered Clavichord,* Book 1, Fugue 20, A minor: "On a bank of mud in the River Nile, on a Sunday morning, a little crocodile sat eating bread and cheese!"

I got to know and to like the older St. Mary's Hill students, who were practicing their languages with me, but I did not get intimate with any of them because of my position—they were pupils and I was their teacher. Among the girls whom I remember was Penelope, called Pop, a red-haired, white-skinned beauty whose style, though not her brains (as Miss Dubochet predicted accurately), got her into Oxford. The pride of the school were the two daughters of Lord and Lady Baden-Powell, the all-potent overlords of British Boy Scouts and their female counterparts, the Girl Guides. The daughters were nice, well-brought-up, and not very bright girls who never did make waves, but who were loved and respected by pupils and teachers alike because of their illustrious parents.

I must have liked St. Mary's Hill from the beginning and fitted in well with the school. What struck me most about England was the politeness with which people addressed each other. I was so used to being shouted at all the time and hearing everybody around me shouting in joy or in anger that the quiet English way of speaking without raising a voice simply floored me. I was also very surprised at the way St. Mary's Hill treated the common cold. In the Italy I knew, common colds were seen as forerunners of pneumonia (before the age of antibiotics) and treated with caution. But here, the sufferer spent the whole day out of doors—warmly dressed, to be sure—studying (or at least carrying her school books) and listening to whatever lessons she could catch through an open window (every window was always kept open, at least a few inches in the winter and all the way up in the summer). At mealtimes, one of the teachers simply piled up a plate with food and pushed it through the dining-room window on the ground floor into the eager hands of the sufferer.

Our food was typical English school food, consisting largely of starches. I remember the Irish stews with their gravy thickened with flour, and the boiled and baked suet puddings. These, contrary to non-British opinion, can be delicious when they are made with a light and practiced hand, as they were at St. Mary's Hill. I remember especially a superb Spotted Dick, studded with raisins, which was boiled for hours in a pudding basin set in boiling water, and Treacle or Jam Tart, where the suet pastry was baked with an ornamentation of jam or treacle, a bland sugar syrup. In England suet, or beef kidney fat, is sold already shredded and ready to use, but here in America, when nostalgia overcomes me, I have to buy my beef fat as it comes, and shred it myself. St. Mary's Hill also spoiled me forever with its rice puddings. These, as Cook told me, her fat arms akimbo on her wide hips, have to be cooked for at least four hours in a slow oven, the formula being one heaped tablespoon of rice, one of sugar, and one quart of cold milk, and never a sullying of raisins or currants. The result is a wonderful, creamy dish that can be eaten either cold or lukewarm.

Sitting in the ground-floor dining room at several tables, each table under the watchful eye of a mistress, we could eat as much as we wanted. But at breakfast and afternoon teatime, we followed a curiously puritanical rule. This was: bread and butter or bread and jam, but never, never bread, butter, and jam together. On Sunday, we were allowed one large, heavy rock cake each.

Another oddity of life at St. Mary's Hill was that everybody had to wear a hat for luncheon on Thursday. The students were stuck with their horrid lids, made of navy plush and sporting a golden yellow ribbon around their graceless crowns. The ribbons, I was told, reflected the color of the school flower, a marigold. As an outsider, I was allowed my own hat, which was on the coquettish side and a present from my father. How the pupils envied me! Why did the whole school, teachers as well as students, wear hats for lunch on Thursdays? Simply to get us used to wearing one when eating in public, where, of course, a lady would never, but never, appear without one. In our nonchalant days, when ladies' hats are a fashion rather than an unavoidable part of a woman's clothes, it is impossible to realize the importance of wearing one at all times, if one was a lady. My Monte Porzio relatives did not mind nearly as much that their house in Rome was located not very far from a *bordello*, as they felt abused by the sight of "these cheap you-know-whats" (to use their words) who wore hats when they went out, "and you know, only a decent woman should wear one."

Neither did I have to wear the school uniform, consisting of the aforesaid hat, a navy overcoat, a navy tunic (wool in winter and cotton during the spring term), worn over a blue blouse and over navy knickers that fastened with elastic at the knees and served as pockets for handkerchiefs and as penwipers. To make the students fit for polite society in their later life, they had to change for dinner every night. Sunday meant a Sunday dress, a more casual one than that worn for dinner.

None of these English ways of doing things did anything but astonish me. They emphasized the sense of strangeness that I have never been able to shed, then or later on, whenever I found myself among Anglo-Saxons in England or in America. But then, as now, I loved every minute of living in England, probably because I never ceased feeling to be an outsider. I think that my not wanting to be English was the reason that the English liked me so much and were kind to me, especially when, so much later, I had married an Englishman and was living in the north of England. Thinking about my life, I have no doubts whatsoever that St. Mary's Hill, intellectually and socially, has had the greatest influence on me; so much so that I shall never cease to be grateful to my old school.

I seem to remember that I did not share the classes of the older pupils, but that I received private lessons from the resident teachers. The school's curriculum, which I also followed, was based upon London Matriculation, which was then the equivalent of A-levels. London Matric showed that you had some in-depth instruction in a number of set subjects. It went further than an American high school diploma, but not nearly as far as the French *baccalauréat* or the German *Abitur* exam. Passing London Matric meant that Oxford or Cambridge would let you take their entrance exams. I do not know if, with London Matric, you could have gone to a lesser university than Oxford or Cambridge, since these two were the only places a gentleman's daughter would want to go, if she went at all to a university. My own coaching for this extremely English exam was quite simple. I had to "do" English history and literature, the Bible, and, in my case, mathematics, which had been a closed subject to me all my life. I remember learning everything about the War of the Roses (forgotten more rapidly than I care to say); studying *Hamlet* so that every word was so familiar as to be repellent; and becoming extremely knowledgeable about the first seven books of the Old Testament. Why these subjects rather than other Shakespearean plays or books of the Bible? As for mathematics, I hated it as much at St. Mary's Hill as I had earlier in Rome. I knew so very little of the subject, which the Roman nuns— quite rightly—had considered unnecessary for girls destined to be wives and mothers. In England I had to work so hard on figures and geometry that I have never been able to get over my hatred of them. All I can say is that, for the first time in my life, I really studied seriously. The joke of it all was that I never took the exam, for reasons I do not remember. What I do remember is that I thought I was pushed to study for London Matric. My instruction had to fit in with the free time of the St. Mary's Hill teachers. I remember especially Miss Athowes, who was very different from Miss Dubochet, whose *alter ego* she had become. I liked this austere and briskly amusing woman who ran the school when Miss Dubochet was away. Poor Miss Athowes had to coach me in mathematics, for her sins, as we both agreed. Miss Raven was a typical elderly, red-nosed British spinster who taught literature; Miss Carr, a small, misshapen lady with Russian connections, was in charge of the school household. These three women, all resident teachers, I knew best among the other mistresses in a school with around a hundred students. Miss Athowes never ate dessert—I still see her peeling an apple at the table. Miss Raven was truly besotted with English poetry and with her brother, Canon Raven, a well-known Anglican priest. Miss Carr owned a charming necklace with four small enameled Fabergé eggs, which had been given to her as an Easter present during a visit to pre–World War I Russia.

Among my papers, I have found two letters that I wrote to my parents from England, which will say more of my life at St. Mary's Hill than I remember now. They are addressed to my father; my mother was traveling. In both letters, I reassured my parents about my well-being. I praised England and St. Mary's Hill, and stressed that I was sorry to have to ask them for some money to buy myself a much-needed coat and shoes, as well as some warm underwear. At the same time, I assured my parents that I would be extremely thrifty and not waste a penny of their money. Then I asked permission to join the school's group of Girl Guides and invest in the Guide's uniform to the tune of about five dollars in today's money. I said that everybody was urging me to join since the two daughters of Lord Baden-Powell, the founder of English Boy Scouts, were my pupils, but that I would never do anything of the kind without my parents' permission. And would they mind if I went on playing hockey and lacrosse? I also wrote that I could not get over the niceness of everybody I met, since I had never known anybody so pleasant and so free of prejudices; that in England old ladies did not exist since the white or gray bobbed heads were as youthful and eager as those of any young person. I described the Misses Dubochet as extremely learned, and yet still human; the milk of human kindness flowed in their veins. They introduced me to all of their friends at their own tea parties, and they were planning "hygienic gymnastics" to improve my posture.

The *au pair* arrangement had proved to be very successful. Apart from having conversation groups mainly in French, I had substituted for the sick French teacher twice, so well that I was going to graduate to full-scale French teaching the next trimester, when the new timetables would go into effect. However, I admitted to a certain amount of homesickness after the first flush of getting acquainted with my new surroundings.

In the year I was at St. Mary's Hill, I lapped up English culture, history, and especially literature like manna from heaven. Miss Dubochet, behind her elegant worldliness, was a very learned woman who had put her private library at my disposal. I read Dryden, Pope, Marlowe, the Restoration comedies, the famous great English poets—Shelley, Keats, Byron, Coleridge, Tennyson, Walter de la Mare, and Rupert Brooke. I developed an intense admiration for Wordsworth; I can still quote many passages from his verse, especially from the sonnets and from his odes. Miss Dubochet taught me to love English nature and lyrical poetry, making me learn long passages by heart. I shall always be grateful to her for doing this; during the frequent bad times of my life, remembering snatches of memorized poetry has comforted me enormously.

However, it was clear that I was Miss Alice's special protégée. Miss Alice's maternal feelings flooded over me and enveloped me in a way that I would never have expected from a stranger. She fussed about my being cold at night and brought me hot lemonade when I had gone to bed, and she made me buy, or herself bought for me, a capacious English hot water bottle. I got very attached to it and admired its passionate pink color. The bottle's fuzzy exterior charmed me especially; it kept my toes from burning. These then existed only in England. Filling one's own hot water bottle was a nightly ritual at Miss Alice's cottage. Around nine o'clock Miss Alice, the students there, and

An early picture of my father, Otto Dittman.

*M*y mother, Maria Leoni, in 1905.

*M*y mother and father in Rome, possibly on their wedding day.

*M*y mother's father, the architect Giacomo Leoni.

My mother's grandmother (with three-month-old Nika on her lap).

(l. to r.) **M**y greatgrandmother, Aunt Matilde, Mother, Uncle Joseph, and Father with me on his lap.

*M*y family, c. 1914 (l. to r.): 1. Aunt Clara Horsch (my father's sister)
2. Clara's husband, uncle Paul Horsch 3. Clara and Paul's daughter,
my cousin Katherina 4. Grandmother Dittman (my father's mother)
5. My father, Otto Dittman   6. Cousin Hilde Horsch   7. Gottlieb Dittman,
my grandfather 8. My mother, Maria Dittman   9. Me

My mother at the Villa Borghese in Rome around 1908.

Aunt Margherita, my mother's sister.

*W*ith my father in Rome, 1920.

At about age four or five in Rome.

*M*y mother's sister Matilde Frank and her husband, Joseph.

A little bit older, in full costume!

*A*rriving in Geneva, 1931.

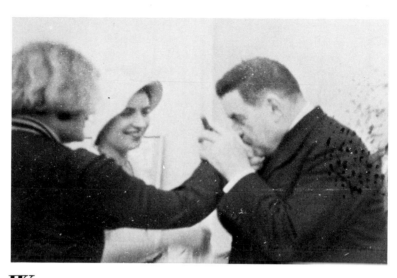

With "le Père Herriot," French representative to the 1932 Reparations Conference in Lausanne.

A view of the beautiful house on Lake Maggiore, in Cerro.

*M*y mother at the house
in Cerro

and my father, in Milan,
1950.

*I*n New York, at Fortune, *I met James Agee.*

Nika, in New York, later in life.

I went into the kitchen to fill our hot water bottles from a gigantic boiling tea kettle. In the year I spent at St. Mary's Hill, summer and winter I went to bed with my beautiful fuzzy hot water bottle. Since, during the winter, the washbasin would freeze most nights, being warm in bed felt doubly wonderful.

When Miss Dubochet started her English lessons with me, oddly enough, with a discussion about Balzac, Miss Alice started taking me regularly with her to the many concerts she went to in Woking and in London. I remember that she was especially fond of Purcell and Elgar, both of whom I considered very English. She also took me to the theater, where I saw Ina Claire in *The Last of Mrs. Cheney.* I don't remember anything about either actress or play, famous as they were. But I remember very well the amateur production of *Dracula* in Woking, where the gentleman-vampire flitted around the stage in tails, covered by a large cape lined in bright red silk. During the Easter holidays, Miss Alice went with me to Eastbourne, on England's south coast, where I learned to love the Downs, and to look over the English Channel from a high cliff, not daring to go too close to its edge, which was brittle, or so I was told. We went to Guildford to visit Dolmetsch, the head of a famous family of musicians and instrument makers, where for the first time in my life I saw a harpsichord and a series of recorders that ranged from the small, light piccolo to the heavy, six-foot bass recorder. Miss Alice also took me to the National and the Tate galleries in London. How it came about I cannot remember, but in the Tate we met Augustus John, the painter, whom Miss Alice admired as an artist and despised as a man for what she called "an irregular way of living." I did not then know what she meant, but I was not sorry to be dragged away from the tall, wild-looking man with the burning eyes. I remembered the eyes and felt afraid, but what of, I do not remember.

I do not think that, in all my life, I had been as happy as I was at St. Mary's Hill. The only disturbing elements were my parents' letters; constantly they told me not to waste any time being a Girl Guide or playing hockey or tennis a couple of hours in the week, but to study, study, study and never to think of anything else but my studies. Once, Miss Dubochet found me in tears after such a letter from home. Not wasting any time, she telephoned Canon Pears, the Church of England parish priest of the church immediately up the hill from the school. The wonderful old man (a relative of Peter Pears, the singer and friend of Benjamin Britten) took me in his study and listened to my anguished sobbings with great patience. Then he told me, very kindly, to stop wallowing in self-pity and to read the Thirty-nine Articles in the Anglican prayerbook. I did this, under his eyes, and agreed with him that they were extraordinary, so much so that I forgot my own misery. From that day, I was convinced, and still am, that if you believe in the Thirty-nine Articles, you can take anything along in your stride. The visit to Canon Pears made me understand the beauty of the old-fashioned English prayer book, and made me go regularly to services in the Anglican church when they were held by Canon Pears. My parents did not care whether or not I went to church, any church for that matter, and the Misses Dubochet had been much too polite to force any kind of religion on me. But I owe one of the great comforts of life to my Church of England school: namely, my love for the English language of the King James Version of the Bible and the prayerbook. I still remember the responses of the Morning and Evening Prayers, and to this day, when in England, I make it a point to hear one or the other in the great cathedrals of Ely, Durham, and Salisbury, which I love best.

I imagine I fitted in so well with St. Mary's Hill life because, not knowing what to expect, I liked everything without restriction. But again, I could not help being bemused by some aspects of school life. The weekly baths were one; the *pot de chambre* and the food are the others I remember best. Outside every bathroom (the loos were separate, as usual in England) hung a typewritten bath schedule for students. It listed a specific time for each one to take a bath. Oddly enough, the bath schedule was not at all limited to before or after school hours. If it was your turn to take a bath, let us say, in the middle of a mathematics lesson, you simply excused yourself with the right reason, took your bath in the allotted fifteen minutes (including dressing and undressing), and came back to your class afterward. The schedules were made new for every school term, and it was one's duty to know when the weekly ablution was due. If you missed your turn, it was too bad; you had to wait for a whole week to bathe again, in the five inches of hot water allotted to each bather. Since I lived at the Cottage, I took my bath down there three times a week, no less, before I went to bed. How I blessed Miss Alice for her largesse with hot water, especially since I could use as much of it as I wanted. I was also bemused by the students' use of chamber pots. Each plain white vessel had its place under each dormitory bed, to be used when need arose during the night. In the morning, when the students had finished dressing, each girl carried her pot to the loo to empty it. To this day, I find the lack of modesty in these corporeal matters astonishing.

As long as I live, I shall be grateful to St. Mary's Hill for having shown me the nice sides of England and for having truly broadened my outlook on life and educated me painlessly at the same time. For better or worse, I can't help judging people and circumstances according to the school's tenets. I would not dare to say this aloud, but when I meet new people, I still ask myself, is he a gentleman or is she a lady?

When in England, long after I had been there as a student, I always looked upon St. Mary's Hill as my home. Miss Alice and I remained close friends. To my surprise, she also became a friend of my mother's, visiting her in Milan several times and, as I found out much later, *en passant,* even inveigling her to take a trip to England. My mother did not like England, however, and I don't think that she ever understood what England has meant to me all my life.

Many years later, I went to see St. Mary's Hill once more. The school did not exist any longer, as I found out on my impromptu visit. But in Horsell's small post office, I was told that the Misses Dubochet could still be found at the Cottage. I still see myself in the drawing room, with Miss Alice aged beyond her years and proud Miss Athowes shrunk into a wizened old woman. Worse still, Miss Dubochet, now totally senile and blabbering, was wheeled into the room by her nurse. Then I fled, weeping.

5. SWITZERLAND

From my childhood on, Switzerland has always been a country where I have felt totally at home. My attachment was fueled by the many casual trips to Lugano, a couple of hours' train journey from Milan. I remember my mother buying herself there a special brand of a unique and superior underwear. My mother's conviction that nothing beats the comfort of a good Swiss hotel, and her staying in such a hotel whenever she could, without me or with me, contributed further to my love for Switzerland. My father also fueled my attachment by bringing me back from his frequent business trips to Bern, the capital, the two kinds of candies I loved best in the world: soft toffees called *Caramel Mou à la Crème* and chocolate mice. The creamy caramels were packed in a little paper box 1¼ inches by 3½ inches (I still have one) that showed, in vivid colors against a range of snowy peaks, a typical Swiss chalet and a few pine trees sitting on a green, flowery Alpine meadow. The large russet head of a melancholy cow gazed upon this Swiss idyll. The cow wore a large collar with the obligatory round cowbell, the kind sold throughout Switzerland as a souvenir. Big, two-toned letters spelled "Kohler," the name of the candy's maker, and some much more subdued lettering identified it as *Caramel Mou à la Crème.* The backside of the little box was not sentimental. It showed an old-fashioned drawing of an immense factory complex: *"Vue Générale de la Fabrique Nestlé, Cailler, Kohler à Broc,"* that is, the names of Switzerland's best-known chocolate manufacturers. *Caramel Mou* were distributed by the Générale des Distributeurs Automatiques, which made it clear that the candy came from a vending machine. The platform of every Swiss train station had at least one of these small vending machines that sold *Caramel Mou* for ten centimes a package.

My parents were not always amenable to giving me the ten-centimes coin for my favorite candy while we were waiting for a train. I had been to Switzerland many times going or coming from one of the high-mountain Swiss resorts my mother liked so much. On one of those trips when, as usual, we had arrived much too early at the station, I had invented a game that yielded every time at least one package of candy. As a train came in from the opposite side, discharging a number of serious business men, I simply ran up to one of them, shouting as loudly as I could: "Papa, Papa!" trying to kiss him as well. Naturally, everybody who saw this display of filial love was touched. The end of this shameful game was always the same: To get himself free in order to flee, the embarrassed victim would get rid of me by thrusting some coins into my hands. Naturally, I ran immediately to the *Caramel Mou* vending machine and got my beloved toffees with the money I just had been given. One day my blackmailing game came to a deserved end. My mother was spending the train-waiting time in the café that is to be found in any self-respecting Swiss train station, while I was out on the platform to con money from unsuspecting traveling gentlemen. This time my victim, anxious to be free, had thrust a whole Swiss franc, in change, into my hands before he fled. A whole franc translated into ten boxes of *Caramels Mou.* As I was pulling the last package from the vending machine, my mother found me.

She had been anxious about me, particularly since the café's waiter had seen me wandering on the platform before our train was due. When she saw the ten packages of candy in my hand, my mother was speechless with anger. She took the toffees from me, threw them in the wastepaper basket provided under each vending machine, amidst my howls, and pulled me into our train, which had just arrived.

My relation to chocolate mice was entirely peaceful and legitimate. Chocolate mice were made of pink or white fondant, and covered with chocolate. Their charm lay in their shape rather than in their ingredients, which were cheap and not very good. These chocolate mice were most realistic, with a curly tail made of string, two eyes consisting of tiny round candies, and a pink snout fashioned of pink sugar. Ah, the joy of biting off a chocolate mouse's head! Ah, the pleasure of biting into the body to find out if it was made of white or pink fondant! Ah, the satisfaction of being left with a curly bit of string to prove that one had feasted on a real mouse! (I had never seen a live mouse, or I might not have been so fond of their candy images.) Chocolate mice were a treat, since each mouse cost ten centimes in a Swiss candy store; only there could they be found in those days in Switzerland. Since I was never allowed to be out by myself and buy chocolate mice with my own pocket money, I felt flattered when a grown-up person bought one or two for me; I felt my taste was accepted by the world of big people. Only once, I remember, did I possess three chocolate mice at the same time, because a Swiss visitor had given them to me. I shall never forget the wonderful feeling of pleasure I had as I contemplated my proud possessions. Now I think that never in all my life has anything pleased me as much as the three chocolate mice I owned for a short, giddy time.

As I said before, Switzerland always felt like home to me, probably because I had been there so often before I came to live in the United States. Switzerland spells total comfort to me, not to mention cleanliness and the fact that everything works in the country, or is repaired immediately when it doesn't behave as it should. In Switzerland, the Swiss leave you alone once you have been allowed into their country, and they invariably do what they say they will do. I never minded that they are reserved and do not go out to make friends with their visitors. Indeed, why should they? And why should they admire our American "out of sight, out of mind" approach to friendship?

When we were in St. Moritz (a resort my mother liked very much indeed), there was the daily excursion to Hanselmann's, one of the world's famous teashops, cafés, *Konditoreien,* restaurants—depending on what you wanted at the time. At Hanselmann's, while my mother sipped her tea, naturally properly made in a pot, and ate a couple of her favorite anchovy canapés, I consumed a pot of hot chocolate and three pieces of cake, one a cream Napoleon, the other two fruit tarts. Everything came with a lovely lot of freshly made, lightly sweetened whipped cream. And to my delighted surprise, hot chocolate, cream Napoleons, and fruit tarts tasted as good to me when, a lifetime later, I went to St. Moritz with my husband and made straight for Hanselmann's. Altogether, as a child, I thought of Switzerland as the ideal country for cakes. I remember Lugano's Huguenin, where an old friend of my mother's conducted me frequently to eat all the cakes I wanted while she drank her *café crème* and listened to the four-man orchestra playing light classical music. In Zurich, there was Sprüngli, where superlative chocolates were made fresh every day, and tasted and cost accordingly. And in Geneva, the Swiss town I came to know best, I could never tire of the *café glacés,* composed of strong coffee, vanilla ice cream, and whipped cream.

I must have been around sixteen years old when I first went to Geneva to study at the Institut des Hautes Études Internationales. I imagine that my parents thought the Institut would familiarize me with the higher international sociology and politics it stood for, but why the Institut, a free university, accepted me, green and raw as a student and a person, I don't know. I surmise the acceptance had a lot to do with the fact that summer schools and their attending students were not to be taken seriously on either side. I remember nothing of my courses, except that the famous Professor Wehberg was my teacher and that I composed for him a very long and learned paper on the subject of the death of Italian liberalism, a subject then of enormous interest to all of Europe. I wrote the original paper in French, the school's and Geneva's official language, but a German translation of it has survived; my father had it translated for his own uses. And I must say, rereading it as I am writing this, it is an excellent paper, explaining the subject well, in clear prose. My thesis was that Italian liberalism would not have dropped dead with Mussolini, that it had a good chance of overthrowing the dictator if it had not been so cowardly in its approach, being much less forceful than Mussolini.

Before I go on, I must speak about the total lack of information about the United States that prevailed in Europe in those days. America was the country where poor immigrants went, unfortunate people who did not have enough to eat at home. Since we had not yet reached the Age of the Common Man, nobody knew these poor devils, all the more since they came from poor southern Italy and from poor Sicily. In all my life, I cannot remember that anybody ever mentioned the United States in any kind of conversation. Thus it came as the utmost surprise to me that I made friends with a number of educated Americans on my first stay here. The lads and girls from the United States must have also been students at the Institut des Hautes Études Internationales, but to me they were fascinating beings from a place I had barely heard of. It does seem incredible now, but one of the young men I went about with was one of the Rockefellers, a name totally new to me. Which one of the Rockefellers it was, I cannot remember. He was a nice, polite young man, as proper as I was, and now I think it must have been a relief for him to go around with a pretty girl who had never even heard of his name.

The person I became friendly with—always very correctly— was a proper Bostonian, with a first name of Greely, which sounded extremely strange to me. I could never understand why he spoke so glowingly of Boston—to my knowledge, a town in England of no particular importance—and praised a university in Cambridge, which I knew to be a college town. When I knew Greely well, I found the courage to ask him to explain his towns to me. For the first time I learned that he was not speaking of places in England, but in the United States of America.

During the middle of the summer, Greely spoke with great pleasure of the forthcoming visit of his second or third cousin, Anthony Standen, a young Englishman who had taken an honors degree in chemistry at Oxford, and who was going to see his American mother in Marseilles before taking off for M.I.T. in Boston. When the young Englishman came, I was greatly taken with his appearance. He was tall, lean, and blond, and he had that unmistakable air of an English gentleman who has been molded by generations of English upper-class birth and education. To add to his charms, Anthony was unselfconscious to a degree I had never encountered before. He spoke rapidly, with a slightly hoarse voice, and he was interested in anything that went on around him; he, Greely, and I were immediately welded into an inseparable trio. On the evening before Anthony was going off to Marseilles, Greely got the notion that he wanted to explore Geneva by night. All night, too. I remember that we were sitting over a late dinner in a cheap restaurant when the American simply got up from the table and took off for heaven knows where. That was the evening when Anthony and I fell in love, wandering up and down in the warm summer night, exploring all the little streets in Geneva's old town, wandering again over the big bridge that spans the Rhone River and unites the two parts of Geneva. Anthony's train was leaving around noon, and in the morning I went around to Greely's apartment where he was staying. I was dumbfounded to find out that Greely had spent the night with a prostitute and was afraid of having caught a disease from her. He had not, and found this out the same day, after his landlady had recommended a doctor to him. (At the time, Geneva was one of the main abortion centers of Europe, and I imagine that the landlady, being used to wayward students, cannot have been very surprised at being asked to recommend a doctor.) We saw Anthony off to Marseilles, and at the station I promised to go down to see him as soon as I could. Which I did, a couple of weeks after, when Greely had gone back to Boston.

I was in love, but also I was anxious to see every sight between Geneva and Marseilles. To finance the trip, I sold a gold bracelet of mine, and took off one evening without a passport, visa, or anything a prudent traveler would normally carry. But I was young and so obviously in love that I managed to get into France without papers. I must have convinced the French immigration officers of the harmlessness of my intentions. Let us remember, this all happened in the second part of the twenties, long before World War II killed both innocence and ignorance. I shall always remember the towering Pont du Gard, which still transported water as it had when the Romans built it; the Roman amphitheater in Nîmes; Tarascon, a town I visited because of its association with one of my favorite books, *Tartarin de Tarascon;* and Avignon, where I sang the famous children's song "Sur le Pont d'Avignon" on the famous bridge. I remember how, in the middle of walking on that bridge, singing loudly, I knew, all of a sudden, that never again in my life would I see those places. I was right.

Anthony's mother lived in a *mas Provençal,* a genuine Provençal house where originally men slept on one side and women on the other. I don't remember anything of the few days that I stayed there, except that once, during our extremely chaste and reserved walks, we danced a little in a bistro where we had stopped for a lemonade. Anthony was going to study at M.I.T., I was going back to Geneva and then to my parents, and the best we could do was to promise to write each other. This we did, but we were both so proper that neither of us even thought it was possible to show affection in our correspondence. After all, we had never spoken of it, let alone shown it in a more tangible way. We wrote each other affectionate, impersonal letters until we got married about three years later. That marriage did change my life, and brought me eventually to the United States. When Anthony decided, after only one month's trial, that he could not bear the state of wedded bliss, and sent me home to my parents in Milan, I was totally crushed. It seemed odd to me to give up a situation after so short a trial, but what could I do but accept his decision and carry on by myself?

Between the late 1920s and the early 1930s, I spent a good deal of time in Geneva. My father had apprenticed me as a secretary–fledgling journalist to an old friend of his who was the head of the Wolff bureau, the official German news agency at the League of Nations, the forerunner of the current United Nations in New York. I was not to live in Geneva, but to go there from wherever I was at the time, whenever I was needed to help report every League event that concerned Germany. In those days, Geneva, the League sessions, and the various big international conferences were the places to be and to be seen. Hordes of people from all over the world descended on Geneva, from international statesmen leading their delegations to journalists of every kind, lobbyists, arms merchants, culture hounds, interested bystanders, and dope peddlers. Geneva was an intoxicating place to be. Though I worked very hard, I did enjoy myself thoroughly, being part of that international melee. Compared to the unsavory (to put it mildly) giant ice cream sandwich on New York City's East River—the United Nations—its predecessor in Geneva was a hotbed of idealism. After all, in those days after the First World War, people still felt that a more peaceful and juster world could be made if one cared—and worked at it. Of course, dirty shenanigans and power politics were going on as they will when nations consort with one another, but it was thought then that international disputes could be solved in a seemingly rational way.

In those days, a long time ago, Geneva was an international city, where people from all over the world came to study and work, or to amuse themselves in a more or less dignified way. Geneva has always been a very beautiful place, with a beautiful lake (called by the natives Lac de Genève and by the rest of Switzerland and all the world Lac Léman or Lake Geneva), breathtaking views of the Alps and Mont Blanc, wonderful promenades, lovely old streets and houses—and the right size, with about 150,000 inhabitants during the thirties. Geneva was a historic town even before the Reformation, which gave the town John Calvin; under him Geneva became for Protestantism what Rome is for Catholicism. As the most important city in French Switzerland, Geneva became, for all intents and purposes, a French town, where French culture and the French language were dominant. We have to think only of the great French figures of the eighteenth century who made Geneva their home—Rousseau, Voltaire, Necker, and Madame de Staël. Geneva was also a haven for political refugees such as Lenin and Bukharin; later, Italian anti-Fascists sought refuge in Geneva as well. In short, Geneva was well suited to become the home of all sorts of international institutions, of which there were sixty-four in the late twenties. However, the native Geneva and the international Geneva (I am talking of the upper echelons of both) only met formally. The Geneva aristocracy, with famous names like that of General Dufour, the founder of the Red Cross, were rich, elegant, cultured, and stuffy people who looked down on even the League of Nations general secretaries and other resident or transient international figures, though they might be equally well born and cultured and stuffy. There were no poor people in Geneva, only lower-class ones, who were rather heavy and solid and, it seemed to me, interested only in eating large quantities of food, such as roast pork with fried potatoes. The *plat du jour* for one in any Geneva restaurant would have been sufficient to feed three hungry people. Whatever their social positions, all Genevois were made for sports of every kind; it was said that a bicycle was as much a Genevois' right as the air he or she breathed. The interesting thing about this elegant and self-possessed quiet town was the enormous number of midwives, whose numberplates graced too many houses to be ignored. All over Switzerland and France Calvin's puritanical town had the reputation of being the best place for "appendicitis" operations. It was no secret that many of the town's elegant first-class clinics drew their large incomes from ladies in embarrassing circumstances, and that Geneva doctors generally had a very helpful attitude toward human erring. Also visible to the naked eye was the disproportionate number of prostitutes, who plied their trade in the old city, where most of Geneva's old families lived in their ancestral homes.

The citizens of Geneva resented the League thoroughly, though they made lots of money from it. The League had taken possession without humility, which prevented the Genevois from feeling humanitarian, as they used to when they gave political asylum to people like Lenin. The Genevois patricians felt slighted, and withdrew completely into their beautiful eighteenth-century houses, full of precious family heirlooms, and into their elegant culture, French-style. They ignored the League officials completely. The ordinary citizen looked upon the newcomers as a financial godsend and made the best of it.

The restaurants in Geneva did well out of the League personnel and the temporary visitors to that institution. The top delegates, with the exception of the French, rarely went out to eat, sticking instead to the very good restaurants of their hotels. The local citizens, elegant or not, ate and entertained at home. But the journalists as well as the lesser League personnel had to go to a restaurant for a change of scenery since Geneva offered few evening amusements. If you knew French well, you might take in a play presented by a visiting company, or you could listen to an occasional concert. If you had the money and means of transportation, you might gamble in Évian, a French enclave on the other side of Lake Geneva. Geneva sported a few nightclubs where you could go dancing, but they were not very reputable ones, and girls taken there were considered fast and loose.

To tell the truth, I was not interested in food at that period in my life, nor in drink, for that matter. (I lived on cheese sandwiches when left to myself.) A very great friend of mine used to take me to lunch in order to get a warm meal into me.

He was a Czech journalist who had been involved in an assassination attempt on Mussolini, and consequently he had to avoid Italy at all costs. Since he was an old-time socialist, he also had to avoid Germany and Austria as soon as the Nazis started rumbling there. There was no way of getting to Prague directly, either by air or by rail, from safe Switzerland. Thus, this poor man used to go home to Czechoslovakia via Denmark and Sweden and Poland; I and everybody else thought this an odd way to travel, though we all saw the necessity of avoiding getting caught and being put to death, after extensive torture, by the Italian Fascists or the German Nazis. How did we know this would happen? From the notices sent out by the Italian and German authorities, which my friend collected and which I read with considerable frissons.

The League of Nations was located in the former Hôtel National on the Quai Wilson on Geneva's left shore. It had been a grand hotel, elegant with the somber pomp of the nineties. (The new League building, farther out in the same direction, had been under construction for years. I never saw it because, when it was finally finished, in 1936, my Geneva years were long over.) The view from the front of the building was magnificent, overlooking Lake Geneva and the Alps in the background. But the back entrance was the one everybody used and where newspapers were sold; I remember that the lady selling the *Christian Science Monitor* had a particularly musical cry.

The general public was not allowed into these hallowed precincts. You had to have a press card, or a delegate's card, and they weren't easy to get. Nevertheless, a lot of strange characters, who were universally called the pests, got cards. The pests were reformers who wanted people to sign petitions—teetotalers, single taxers, and a lot of quite sweet, elderly American ladies who felt strongly on women's suffrage, peace petitions, narcotics, and the white slave trade. Journalists blanched at their sight and fled.

Converted bedrooms and bathrooms housed all the League personnel. The ex-hotel's public rooms had been adopted for committees, of which there were a great many. When the space at the League turned out to be inadequate for major events, such as the Disarmament Conference, a modernistic building, known as the Disarmament Building, was built by the town of Geneva to house them. The new building, connected by a passage to the old League in the former Hôtel National, housed also the *Salle des Pas Perdus* (the Hall of the Lost Steps, if a literal translation is wanted). The *Salle,* a passage about a couple of hundred yards long, was *the* place where delegates and journalists met and talked, where you saw everybody at one time or another. In short, it was *the* place to be. One end of the *Salle* was lined with huge glass cases filled with millions—I think it was five million, no less—of peace petitions from all over the world; each petition was tied with a length of red ribbon. Most of them came from England and the United States. Nobody ever paid the slightest attention to the petitions, an indication of the futility of so much human endeavor.

The world of the League of Nations was basically divided into three classes. One was composed of the steady employees—a kind of international civil service, which included the boss of it all, the secretary general of the League, as well as the lowliest typist. The second was the accredited-to-the-League delegations, augmented in important times by temporary delegations which had come to Geneva for specific meetings. The third was the hordes of international journalists accredited to the League. The journalists either lived in Geneva and reported on the League all the year round or they came, like a number of the delegates, for specific League meetings. Around these official groups spun a galaxy of onlookers, some of whom, like Lord Beaverbrook, were important and had political influence.

The League people, on the whole, were not outgoing. The first secretary general, Sir Eric Drummond, set a really heroic pattern of inhospitality, which was followed by his lessers. Most League officials of their own rank got a hurried *"bonjour"* as they swept in or out of meetings, while lesser delegates and journalists met frozen stares. No big English delegate ever walked alone either. He always had a bodyguard of tall, well-dressed young men around him, to protect him from the world. The English hated to give interviews, they hated leaving their hotel. British delegates never ate out like the French, whom you could find every night in one of the excellent Geneva restaurants. I remember looking at Sir Austen Chamberlain in one of the meetings and thinking how curious it was that he had a wife, who presumably kissed him sometimes. I tried to imagine what it would be like, but I couldn't.

Two determined ladies, though, had managed to overawe the English delegates—American Mrs. Bullard and English Mrs. Barton. Each was what is called "a fine figure of a woman." Both wanted to be political hostesses and were rivals in lion catching. Mrs. Barton had a reputation of really exquisite rudeness. The story went around that she once sent a dinner invitation to Elihu Root which went, by mistake, to a young Englishman by the name of Root. He turned up but Mrs. Barton, seeing he was the wrong Root, told him in front of all her other guests, "I didn't want you, you had better leave at once."

Mrs. Bullard, on the other hand, wanted more. She had managed to get herself elected to an American delegation that was observing something or other, since America was not a League member. She clung to John L. Lewis, the labor leader and the delegation's most prominent member. It was told how, at one meeting, where she burned with indignation at what everybody was saying, she whispered to him, "I just don't know what to do. I feel I *must* go up and make a speech." Lewis said loudly, "It's their show, sister, you keep out of it."

But such was the forcefulness of these two ladies that no English delegate, however high up, would have dared refuse their invitations.

A man who created a stir because of his inherited wonderful Japanese-Austrian looks was the Count Richard Coudenhove-Kalergi, who had thought of and promoted Paneuropa, a truly European alliance—a novel idea in those days—which would bring universal peace. I wonder if anybody took the rather superior-acting count very seriously, apart from some League biggies, such as Briand, who granted him a hearing. The old Aga Khan wandered about, very serious and very large; we all wished we were the recipients of the gold he fetched from his religious followers when they weighed him each year. He was in the habit of giving one large party for the delegates of the various nations who were accredited to the League, for which he issued invitations reading, *"Messieurs les Délégués et les Dames qui les accompagnent,"* which translates into, "delegates and the ladies who are with them." The old *viveur* knew the ladies were, at best, mere secretaries. A Rumanian lady delegate—short, fat, plain, and badly dressed—was fond of excusing her running around *"comme un papillon, je voltige de feuille en feuille,"* (like a butterfly, I tumble from leaf to leaf).

Actual League meetings, big and small, took place in suitable rooms, but the *Salle des Pas Perdus* was the place where delegates, journalists, and onlookers met constantly, talking to each other without attracting undue attention. An important part of this true meeting place of the world's most diversified opinions was Carlo's Bar, where everyone always ended up. Carlo was a dark and sleek Italian, with plenty of understanding and an equal amount of discretion. The celebrities who confided in him would make the owners of publicized New York nightclubs sick with envy. In the morning, Carlo dispensed orange juice and Vichy water. The Balkans and South Americans were his best customers for these wholesome refreshments, because they couldn't keep up with the French, English, and Americans (who drank cocktails and hard liquor all day long). The British had the reputation of drinking beer, with brandy and soda between beers. Carlo's bar was also a general refuge during translation time; every speech had to be translated into the two official languages, French and English. During translation time, every delegate who could get out of the meeting did so to congregate at Carlo's Bar; if he could not get away, he would try to sleep like Briand and Lord Cecil. Not only politics were hotly discussed at Carlo's Bar, but many private relations of a delicate nature as well. Carlo's bar was a great place for flirting and for assignations. For people who wanted a little privacy, there were small cubicles, furnished with uncomfortable steel chairs and steel tables. I remember one big-time League session when, in the middle of the morning, I drank Vichy water with a somber Yugoslav delegate, whose name I have forgotten. The melancholy Slav made a great impression on me since he constantly complained about the sadness of life. I also remember being smiled at by the ferocious and satanic-looking Indian politician Krishna Menon, whose nonverbal benevolence frightened me no less than his nationalist reputation. In the *Salle des Pas Perdus*, I interviewed the U.S. secretary of state, Mr. Stimson, who was not amused by being asked by me to talk about America's plans for the future of Germany. No wonder Mr. Stimson felt miffed; he had never given an interview to a German journalist before.

It was part of my job to telephone the League news to Berlin as soon as the report had been dictated to me by my boss, or as soon as I had written up the less-important League doings myself. Any news agency journalist was constantly competing with the representatives of the big and small dailies who had to come to Geneva; in those days, all communications were by telephone since cable news was sent only to overseas papers. Since it was always imperative to get through to one's home office as quickly as possible, the telephone room was just off the *Salle des Pas Perdus*. The telephone room held about thirty-five or forty booths, and was manned by mature "girls" who took no nonsense from anybody. It was used almost exclusively by journalists; the delegates, more refined and less hurried than the press, used to make their calls from their own offices. One generally placed calls by yelling the number at those formidable Swiss "girls." When the connection was ready, the "girls" would chase you in the *Salle des Pas Perdus* or even in a meeting. For obvious reasons, being on excellent terms with the telephone ladies was of paramount importance. When they liked you, and knew that something special was going on at the League, they would put your call through on their own. Thus, by the time you got out of your meeting, your call was ready for you or would come in a few minutes. Even the nastiest journalists knew that the telephone ladies could make one's life happy or miserable, so they went out of their way to be polite and agreeable. All the journalists knew that it was desirable to present the telephone ladies with candy or money, especially at Christmastime. Once, having spent over an hour dictating my report to the Berlin home office, I figured out that in rush times an agency journalist would spend as much as five hours a day in a telephone booth.

In spite of all the political talk in my home, I was incredibly naïve and personally uninterested in League politics, as these two episodes will show. And I don't think that either would have happened had I not been the pretty, insouciant child I was in those days.

One day, I'd been sent to the Hôtel des Bergues to get the press handouts from the French delegates who lived there. I had to wait, and sat down in the lobby. A portly, full-faced gentleman sat next to me and in no time at all, I told him the story of my life. He then gave me tea and bought me a box of candy. I couldn't have been more surprised when I saw him the next day in one of the meetings. He was Mackenzie King, lately the Canadian premier, who had always refused to talk to any German journalist.

There was another great man, the greatest of them all, who honored me with his friendship—Briand, the French politician. He was at the height of his career, and was leading the French delegation in Geneva. He was small, shabbily dressed, with a straggling moustache, and an unlighted cigarette dangling from the corner of his mouth most of the time. Briand was the champion of an understanding with Germany, a realistic, practical one. If he had lived, the Second World War might never have been.

Briand was easily amused at what went on around him, and he had a truly French contempt for pomp and circumstance. Quite often, he broke away from his entourage to talk to somebody, whether he knew him or not. I presume my air of utmost innocence in that sinful League atmosphere must have amused him, because he came up to me one day as I was standing around, and asked me to have a glass of grenadine at a little bar across the street. After that he talked to me quite often, but never about politics. We talked about literature, the philistine character of many Swiss, the various Paris exhibitions, life in England, which he considered dreary; I wish I had kept a diary. He also took me to luncheon several times—good ones, because he loved to eat. We went to the Simplon, a place famous for its *hors-d'oeuvre,* just the two of us, with an agent of the Geneva police somewhere in the background. The proprietor would greet us with a *"Bonjour, Monsieur le Ministre.* A table for Monsieur and Madame, Jean," or whatever the waiter's name was. And then the great man would ply me with food and laugh at my prattle.

It never occurred to me to make any professional capital out of this relation. I am sure that if I had, the whole thing would have been off. My boss told me later that when he asked me one day if Briand had said anything about the subject that was foremost in everybody's mind in those days, French-German relations, I drew myself up haughtily with, "I never mix my personal life with business."

In Germany the Nazis were rumbling louder and louder. The Wolff bureau news agency was still not affected by them, but we noticed that the German delegates were. The haughty and pallid von Papen was a German delegate who was definitely trimming his sails to the wind by being uncooperative to the Wolff bureau. The question of Germany's reparations for her role in the First World War was a great point of dissension. The French, for obvious reasons, wanted the Germans to pay and pay, both morally and with money. Those contentions that began with the Versailles Treaty, festering in all of Europe's minds, led to long forgotten international conferences like the 1932 Reparations Conference in Lausanne. After endless discussions, the matter was to be settled at last. At least the nations tried to settle their problems in a peaceful manner, which is more than what happens so frequently today. But at the time I am writing about, the world, or some of it, still thought that the 1914 war should, and even might, be the last one.

The Reparations Conference in Lausanne on Lake Geneva attracted worldwide attention, and hordes of extra delegates and journalists descended on the city. I believe the German negotiator was von Papen, and I know that the French one was M. Herriot, "le Père Herriot," as the French premier and exmayor of Lyons was called; he was very popular in France as a solid bourgeois with a visible fondness for good food and wine. I was in my element flitting equally from French to British to German delegations to sound them out, and the Wolff bureau was happy about it because I could talk to them in their own languages, more than my boss was able to do. When the accord between France and Germany was reached, it was negotiated largely with native shrewdness by the wily M. Herriot, who had few if any illusions about *"la vie,"* as he liked to say. We all knew, including the Germans, that his lack of illusions included any concerning Germany's feelings and intentions. Who was to blame him or, for that matter, Germany, busy with the increasing role of the Nazis? On the day the final agreement was consolidated, M. Herriot appeared in the crowded delegates' passage and beckoned me to him. A young French woman journalist, representing a major newspaper, was already standing at his side. With a sweep of his arms, he drew both of us to him, soundly kissed each of us, and declared words along the lines of "to the new French-German understanding." Both of us girls were pleased with the applause and thought nothing more of it. At least I presume the Frenchwoman, under her tricot cap (I remember what she looked like and that her first name was Claude), thought nothing of it; but I was not allowed to ignore it. All hell broke loose in the Nazi German press about this Frenchman's ravaging of a German maiden's honor. Official threats were sent to the German delegation that the least they could do was to fire me and also take it out on my family in Milan. I knew little and cared less about the brouhaha until it came to my ears that the British and American journalists had bonded together to save me by telling the German delegation that if they yielded to pressure, they, the British and American journalists, would splash the whole affair on their front pages to an extent that would harm Germany seriously. The Germans left me alone after all of this, but my relations with German delegates and the already, with few exceptions, servile German press, became even cooler. But the story does not finish here. Some weeks after the event, a French secretary whispered to me to come on a certain day and hour to Geneva's most luxurious Hôtel des Bergues because M. Herriot wanted to see me. I was pleased with the invitation, but when I got in the little hall that separated the French premier's suite from the hotel corridor, an agitated young man showed me into a closet, hissing, "Stay here as long as I tell you!" I could not help peering out, and lo and behold, Herr von Papen emerged on his way out from M. Herriot's room. It certainly would never have done for him to find me, an official German journalist, on my way to see the "French fiend," as some of the German press called M. Herriot. The French premier received me with utter friendliness. We conversed at length about myself, and as I was leaving he presented me with several yards of the most exquisite silk from Lyons, his beloved hometown, which I got made into a smashing dress. The silk was blue because M. Herriot thought I would like the color, which indeed I did.

Apart from the *Salle des Pas Perdus*, journalists met in the Bavaria, an ordinary Genevois brasserie that became famous and immensely popular after Briand, Stresemann, and Sir Austen Chamberlain had been there in the years 1927–1928. Around ten at night, the journalists began drifting in to socialize with each other, to drink beer, and also to find out if they had missed anything they should have reported on. Younger secretariat people and diplomats also went to the Bavaria, which was *the* place to be after ten in the evening. Visitors to Geneva were taken to the Bavaria as a matter of course and sat there, simply overwhelmed with international life. I remember taking my mother to the Bavaria after a performance at the Geneva Casino by Josephine Baker, who had danced dressed only in a bunch of bananas stuck in her rear end. My mother did not enjoy either Josephine Baker or the Bavaria, especially when she noticed that journalists seemed to get perturbed when one or the other rushed to the telephone for a late call. Deadlines occurred around midnight, and they were afraid of having missed out on some event or other. My mother was not taken either with the informality of it all, seeing how everybody table-hopped all the time.

There are dozens of inns like the Bavaria in any Swiss town or village. But this one had transcended its humble status as a purveyor of beer, potatoes, and kraut. Beer was still the liquid most often drunk because it was cheap and good. I seem to remember that the Bavaria beer was blond rather than dark. With the beer, the journalists consumed quantities of cooked sausages served with home-fried potatoes and stewed cabbage or sauerkraut. The Bavaria also provided more elaborate fare. One could get veal cutlets there, fried whole or cut into strips to make the famous Zurich specialty *Geschnetzeltes;* the veal strips are cooked and finished with a cream sauce in a most tasty manner. One could also get pork chops fried with apples and onions, and thick soups as well, made from dried peas or lentils. In other words, the place provided good, solid home cooking that went with either beer or the local wine from the upper lake and from the Canton Valais. The wine was generally white and called Goutte d'Or (Golden Drop); it resembled our Chardonnay. It was not expensive; the red wine cost more since it came from famed cellars throughout Switzerland, where the red wines of the Rhone Valley are prized. Good Swiss wine is seldom found in America, but I know from my own later experience in Switzerland, and from what connoisseurs told me, that the red Rhone wines were a cross between the French Burgundies and the Hermitage wines of the River Rhone.

As everywhere in Switzerland at that time, the food at the

Bavaria was served in serving dishes and kept warm on hot plates that, stacked together prior to use, were connected with an electrical outlet to keep them hot. The server served a first helping, then, if you wanted more food, it was up to you to get it from the serving dish on the hot plate, deposited in front of you on the table. This way, the food was always hot and tailored to the amounts you wanted. I have never been able to understand why even the fanciest American restaurants have to serve you a determined portion ready on a plate when it would be so simple to adopt the Swiss way of serving food. No restaurant owner has been able to explain to me the fixed amount serving on an individual plate, especially before the advent of *cuisine nouvelle*, which requires a display as picturesque as it is mannered. Interestingly, *Teller* service, that is, one single portion of food brought to you on a plate, cost much less than the other kinds, and it was also to be found in cheap restaurants.

The serving at the Bavaria was done by women dressed in black with white aprons; they were called *Serviertöchter* (serving daughters). At the time, even in posh places, few waiters were employed since the Swiss habit was for *Serviertöchter.* These ladies, young or old, were extremely respectable and known to be so. The young servers usually came from a hotel or restaurant background; before going into the business at home, they had learned its ins and outs somewhere else. There must have been some canoodling going on with these ladies, but never have I known a man brave enough to trifle with a Swiss *Serviertochter.*

Always very much in evidence at the League and in every kind of international social scene were two Hungarians, both internationally famous caricaturists, who had made their fame at the League with their extremely skillful and equally witty caricatures of all present. Derso was tall, reserved, and on the melancholy side; Kelen also was tall, good-looking, and outgoing, and always looking, looking. He knew everything that went on. He ended up at the United Nations in New York doing UN radio; Derso was dead by then. Derso and Kelen produced for the French periodical *Le Rire,* and people could buy their stuff, including a collection of masterful Geneva caricatures, *"Le Testament de Genève, ou 10 années de coopération internationale,"* which I still have and cherish. They were kind to me, and never caricatured me, which would have been very easy; I was grateful. But, oh, how some people, especially the VIPs, hated to see themselves in precarious and funny ways, such as dancing around the Golden Calf of International Finance or climbing naked out of trees in scenes of Paradise. Both Derso and Kelen had very sharp eyes and were fine artists, and the climate of the times was such that everybody could be caricatured. Imagine what would happen now if the big shots and journalists of the current UN were ridiculed—a thought that does not bear thinking.

The journalists were a motley crowd. Among those I remember especially is Lus, a Dutch girl of androgynous beauty, with short blond hair cut like a boy's and extremely thick; she kept her figure by never eating lunch, but she drank it and was known for her love of strong waters and wine. She was the ultimate charmer, anything but an intellectual. She had painted her apartment walls all in black, which was considered very daring, and I remember her telling me that putting your blouse collar over your jacket or sweater was tacky; the proper way is never, but never, to show your collar. To this day I never pull out a collar. Lus ended up by marrying, years later, a melancholy and supersensitive, superaesthetic, and rather supercilious Thai delegate who had been her suitor for years; no one was surprised at the combination.

Lus Hartman's great friend was the American journalist Mary Lloyd, a witty and generous woman who was first cousin to the then famous Maury Maverick of Texas, known to all at that time for his support of the New Deal and many liberal causes. Two other American journalists of the coterie stand out in my memory: James Whittacker, elegant and playful and married for a short time to Mary Lloyd, and Stewart Brown, a tall, rangy man married to Helen, a very pretty and very charming woman. Stew Brown had been UPI correspondent in Rome and enjoyed a reputation as the best American reporter. He was a strong, silent character who later committed suicide. I heard this long after I had lost touch with Geneva people. His desolate wife, I also heard, finally married somebody else and went to live in San Francisco. I shall always think with great affection of Stew and Helen Brown, both of whom struck me, even in my then complete ignorance of Americans and their ways, as totally lovable and admirable people. I still practice Helen's way of topping a green salad with thinly sliced red radishes, which looked great and tasted good after the radishes had been tossed into the salad at the table.

I remember James Whittacker most for a story he once told about the Spanish Civil War that still makes me shudder. It seems that he was sitting outside a Moorish barracks with the commandant of the Moorish brigade (on Franco's side) when a soldier brought in two young women who had been caught on the Republican side. When the guard turned them over to the Moorish commandant, Whittacker heard a long, loud sigh echo from the barracks. "They will last only a few hours when my soldiers get through with them," he said to Whittacker, nodding to the guard to take his two young prisoners into the barracks and let the Moorish soldiers loose on them.

It was interesting to see how the journalists had grouped themselves. On the whole, French stuck with French, as did English with other English; they mistrusted all other writers, especially those from the smaller nations. At that time, the German and Russian journalists were reasonably close to each other, as were some of the delegates. The reason for this was the usual one at that time: when Nazism in Germany started rumbling openly, the only counteraction to it that seemed possible was from the extreme left—in other words, Russia. Added to this was the cultural factor that Russians and Germans shared; all educated Germans admired Dostoevsky and Gorky. What's more, French and Anglo-Saxons seldom, if ever, spoke anything but their own languages, and the Russians were fluent in German rather than in French or English.

I must have met the Russian journalists through my room-mate Millie, who worked at the League in some minor job. Millie, very pretty and very American, had first canoodled with the son of the great Spanish composer Albéniz, who was an arms merchant in Geneva. (Later on I thought, what better place for an arms merchant than Geneva?) When Millie and I roomed together, her boyfriend was Romm, the Russian correspondent of *Tass*, the official Russian news agency. Romm was rather mysterious about himself, though friendly enough to Millie and me. He often came to see us, bringing exotic food which we cooked for him. He was not at all a drinking, backslapping Russian, nor did he ever talk to us about Russia and Communism. (Years later, I heard that he got caught in one of the Moscow purges, and that he confessed his Trotskyist guilt.) I remember Romm teasing me for wearing a girdle, which he had found out by putting a friendly arm around me. He lectured me on the discouraging effects girdles have on the male sex, though I assured him that this was not necessarily so at all. I also shall never forget how Romm, leading Millie to the bathroom for her douche, invariably said, *"après l'amour, l'hygiène."*

The first Russian I ever met in my life was Constantine Oumansky who, years afterward, became ambassador to Washington, and later died a mysterious death in Mexico. Whether or not he was a master Machiavelli when he came to this country, I do not know, since I never saw him or any of the other Russians I knew outside Geneva. There he just seemed a rather tense young man, who hardly ever talked about politics, but about art, for which he cared a lot.

I had done my day's work and was about to go home when this unknown, short, slight man approached me in a state of great agitation. "I need company," he said, "my wife is having a baby in Moscow, and I am terribly nervous. Come and have supper with me."

That night was the only time he ever talked about himself. He had run away from home at fifteen to join the revolution, and he had written a book about modern painting and was contemplating another. And now his wife was having her first baby and he didn't know what to do.

"Let's go and send her a telegram," he proposed. We did. Then we went for a walk and sent another telegram. Then we rode in a cab and sent yet another telegram. Then we had coffee somewhere and sent another telegram. By the time I was through, we had sent about two dozen wires. But Mrs. Oumansky must have been very engaged in her labors; her husband learned about four days later that he had a daughter.

The star of the Russian journalists was Karl Radek, who had had a very agitated career as a revolutionary and as a politician, and who later perished in one of Stalin's purges. The first time I met Radek he was talking to Carl von Wiegand, the Hearst Press correspondent and an important man. Everybody was looking at the small, slight man dressed in a gray Russian army tunic without insignia; he never dressed in any other way. Radek was quite exceptionally ugly, but one forgot his looks when he spoke. He was very frank and very witty, and spoke rapidly and with animation. Radek liked me, and he explained to all and sundry that his liking was based on my abysmal ignorance of what was going on around me. Those were his very words, I remember.

Radek wore false teeth and he had a trick to make me laugh, pushing out the upper plate. Whenever he saw me trying to get information out of some delegate, taking diligent notes, he would push out his plate and make faces at me. He did it too when he was sitting in on meetings and I was listening on the press benches. Each time my composure would be gone completely.

Radek had a reputation for improper stories. Nothing shocked me more, as all my friends knew. So, whenever I came near him entertaining a group of people, he would clap his hand on his mouth and say, "Whatever I do in life, I must not shock Nika. Let's speak of clean things now."

It was Radek who introduced me to the hoary game of beaver. Any man with a beard is a beaver, and you count beavers the same way you score in tennis. Whenever we couldn't shout gleefully at each other that we had seen a new beaver—those we saw every day didn't count—we used to go into awful contortions communicating the happy find. I once conveyed to Radek, entirely by signs, that I had seen a beaver diving into the lake from a boat. He was a white-haired one at that, which was better than a brown beaver, but not as good as a red-haired one. The game was carried on throughout the whole Disarmament Conference, with telegrams if we could not reach each other any other way. It died a natural death after Radek came back from a short trip to Moscow. There, in a hospital, he had seen, so he swore to me, a five-year-old girl with a long black beard. I could never hope to top this ne plus ultra of beavers, and I gave up, crushed.

The futility of so much human endeavor is clearer than ever when one thinks of all the journalists who, at one time or another, really worked their tails off at the League of Nations. The journalists came in all degrees of importance and respectability. The correspondents of the big London and Paris dailies, as well as the correspondents of the official news agencies, were at the top of the hierarchy. Then there were the glamour boys, people like Sinclair Lewis, Will Rogers, and other international luminaries, who swooped down to write "think" pieces. Every regular journalist hated them because they insisted on wanting to meet important personages who, most of the time, shrank from being interviewed. At the bottom of the list were the so-called correspondents we all avoided at any cost, who represented such publications as the Lower Slobodia Bee Keeper's Journal or the Women's Club Associations of rural Somaliland.

Where are all the journalistic celebrities now? And who remembers their names?

6. ENGLAND, BERLIN

I once figured out that in the last ten years before I came to the United States I never spent more than three to four months in the same place. This is not as glamorous as it may sound, because the places where I spent so little time then were always the same, i.e., London, Berlin, Geneva, and Italy. I was restless, but obviously the failure of my marriage and turmoil of Europe encouraged my restlessness rather than restrained it; in other words, I was at a complete loss as to what to do with my life. Unfortunately, my inability to remember what happened when has forced me to describe my life in terms of people and places rather than in a proper chronological order.

Thinking back, I realize that my future was shaped in equal amounts by the later failure of my marriage in England and by the coming of the Nazis in Germany. And of course the constant leitmotif of my life was that I had to work to support myself. Since I loved England better than any other country I knew, I went to London, where I knew my way around and from where it was possible to see Anthony Standen; he was working as a chemist in the big ICI (Imperial Chemical Industries) plant in the north of England.

I had started college, the London School of Economics, between trips to Geneva, Berlin, and Italy. All in all, I spent a little less than three years at LSE, and I was thinking of settling down to get my degree when my big chance, a job in New York, turned up. There was no time for me to do anything but decide to accept this job. I gave up any thought of a London School of Economics degree and, in all fairness, I must say that not being a college graduate has never bothered me professionally to this day.

I went to the London School of Economics because of my interest in social and economic problems. It was famous for its founder, Sir William Beveridge, for its teachers, and for its interest in international affairs. LSE was in London, a city where I felt confident that I could earn a living. To this day, I cannot understand why I was accepted for a degree by LSE; I had spoken frankly about having to work in Geneva and not being able to be in London without interruptions; but accepted I was, without trouble. I registered for late afternoon and/or evening courses, which left me free to work for money during the day. This is not the place to tell at length about the turmoil and other war legacies that beset England at that time. LSE was progressive and up-to-date, in those days known as a very liberal and somewhat leftist institution, while Oxford and Cambridge appeared to be fossilized, and they were the only two universities that counted to the people I went around with.

The teachers, from the head Sir William Beveridge down, included many well-known English political figures. Hugh Dalton was a minister, and Ellen Wilkinson was a Labour member of Parliament. But it was Harold Laski who made the greatest impression on me and from whom I learned to think more clearly, and to be more accurate and specific about my words. Harold Laski was a small, vivacious man who liked his students sufficiently to invite them for Sunday afternoon tea in his house in North London. His memory was spectacular and accurate down to the last detail. When Laski said that on July 23, 1127

(I am making this up to illustrate my words), this or that thing happened with so and so, you could be sure that the little professor was right. At first, no student would believe him, but at Laski's invitation we checked his facts many, many times, only to find that he was always correct. Whether one agreed with Laski's ideas or not, one could not help learning a lot from him. Laski was a wonderfully stimulating teacher who delighted to confront his students with paradoxes and contradictions, which he asked us to solve. But he had to teach personally, at *viva voce;* as a writer he was dull and uninspiring, which is perhaps the reason that he is remembered not as a writer, but as a personality. He himself knew that his personality, rather than his beliefs, was paramount in his teaching; we discussed the subject many years later, when I saw him in New York.

Since I had other interests in London, I never got as entangled with the students as one would normally. First of all, LSE was not a college with its own life, but a place where one went to lectures; none of the people I knew there was interested in college activities, though I presume some such things must have existed. My background and my political work in Geneva, in a way, chose my friends for me, and thus I consorted with Jewish students who were actively or passively interested in the liberation of Palestine. I only remember one of the Jewish students personally and by name, possibly because I saw him later in New York, where he loved corn on the cob so much that he ate it for breakfast: Moishe Perlman, who I heard later became the press officer of the Israeli government. Moishe, who frequently was very cross, was cheerful and patient with me, and he knew a lot of interesting people. I remember that he once took me to a small left-wing bookshop not far from LSE, which was on a small street off Holborn, to meet one of his pals, called Esmond Romilly (nephew of Lady Churchill, later the husband of Jessica "Decca" Mitford). None of us was very soigné in those days, but this wild-eyed, passionate, tousle-haired youth looked worse than any of my friends. But, oh, did he speak with an upper-class accent! He combined it with extremely left-wing attitudes in what I now know to be a typically English manner. The three of us had supper together in a cheap student café (pronounced "caf") where we discussed, of all things, the famous saying of Alice Delysia, a popular actress of the time: "There are only two ways to keep a man. One, if you really are a super bitch, you can outbitch any other woman. But if you are not, and super bitches are rare, the only way to keep your man is to make him super comfortable, since super comfortable men do not stray." Delysia, who was well known for her gentlemen friends who bestowed affection and largess on her, was also known to be a kind woman, I may add.

I have a vivid memory of another of my LSE pals, an Ethiopian who, unlike myself and my other friends, *was* extremely soigné in his appearance. I do not remember his name, but he told me that his father, a cousin of Ras Tafari (Haile Selassie), the emperor of Ethiopia who later took his troubles with the Italians to the League of Nations, had been imprisoned for many years in a dungeon by the emperor himself. He insisted that I understand this unloving imperial attitude towards a relative as something felt by all Ethiopian emperors when they did not like a relative or were jealous or afraid of him. My Ethiopian admirer wore light gray flannel suits; the jacket seams were picked out with dark gray stitching. But his true glory was his black beard; it was simply magnificent—glossy, thick, and on the curly side, cut square and reaching halfway to his chest. In those days, young men did not wear beards. When he was asked why he did wear such a splendid specimen, he answered simply that it was customary in his country for young gents to be bearded. Never having been to Ethiopia, none of us could question his words, but the old saying "oiled and curled like an Assyrian bull" was true in the Ethiopian's case. As for me, never again in my life have I encountered so splendid a beard.

Over the years, I had diverse jobs in London. Among them— they all lasted for a short time—was being a secretary to Mr. Alexander Korda, the proud and haughty movie mogul who was then just getting big in the English cinema. I remember nothing of this particular enterprise of mine except that I once took a parcel of his to the post office and that I was struck by the address, Tewkesbury, a place I had never heard of.

At one time, I was a fish shop helper in Clerkenwell, the district near the Smithfield meat market, which then was strictly lower-class; for all I know, it may now be gentrified beyond recognition. I had gone to Smithfield market to visit a butcher—the father of a fellow student—to collect something for a number of us who used to cook together, and I must have looked rather pitiful, for the man asked me if I was down on my luck, as indeed I was. "Go there and there," he said to me, "but go immediately to see this friend of mine who has a fish shop in Clerkenwell. He needs help in the shop because his wife is ill." He said—and I'll forever remember his words—"You look as if you can take it."

I ended up in a narrow side street, dark as sin and as unsavory as most sins, illuminated by a miserable gaslight. The shop was a hole in the wall, selling fish and poultry (read: rabbits) to the poor in the neighborhood. The owner was a nice Cockney. Since I was about to be thrown out of my bed-sitter for nonpayment of rent (one guinea a week with breakfast), I took the job he offered me, wages amounting to eight shillings a week, with bed and board. That is, I slept in the bed with his wife, while he slept in the kitchen.

The first evening I had to scrub the shop from top to bottom, which was, I assure you, not a poetical job. The people themselves were by no means dirty, but since the woman had been sickly for months she was incapable of doing much around the house, let alone the shop. She spent her days sitting upright, totally silent, in the kitchen, and came to life only once a day, or rather night. After pub closing, her husband used to come back drunk from the neighborhood salon, usually with female company to whom he would bid fond and lengthy adieus at his front door. Then the wife became a raging fury, shouting and cursing and throwing anything she could lay hands on at her husband's head. It soon became clear to me why the husband had asked me to lock up all the dishes, pots, and pans, and to give him the keys to the cupboard. In the morning he returned the keys to his wife, as if nothing had happened. The neighbors were used to those nightly scenes and thought nothing of it; on the contrary, my employers were considered to be a happy couple.

Both were very good to me. We had plenty of food, cooked largely by myself and a neighbor, and they asked me no questions after I told them that I was on my own. There were enough people around for them to wonder about, and I was a good worker. I used to get up at five in the morning, after having slept solidly in the joint bed; the woman let me have the larger part of it because "you work hard, dear." The husband had already been to the market by that time, and we had to prepare the fish, the chickens, and the rabbits for the shop. Of these activities, skinning the rabbits was the most hateful. They look like babies when skinned, and it makes one feel like Herod. We drank innumerable cups of strong tea as we worked and discussed politics; the man used to tell me of his British army experiences, which had been brutal. He could not understand why the many unemployed who begged for our throwaway scraps did not make a revolution but instead, like himself, tried to get as drunk as they could as often as they could pay for it. "It's the quickest way out of Clerkenwell," he used to say.

The evenings were the worst because the shop had to be scrubbed. There is nothing more depressing than the dead look of fish heads; and after a sixteen-hour working day, cleanliness becomes a relative matter. On Saturday night we washed ourselves in the kitchen—though not at the same time, I hasten to say, because we were very proper people. On Sunday I stayed in bed until noon and went to see my friends in the afternoon. They were not surprised by my life, and I rather liked it myself. I think for the very first time I felt necessary to somebody and part of the working world.

Meantime, my absence from the London School of Economics had been observed and frowned upon by my teachers. As they planned to kick me out if I did not return, and as this would have meant I would have to leave London, I returned to my studies. I had an obvious excuse: a cut on the finger that swelled up and became nasty. But my employers would not have let me go because of this—they knew what it was to need the money. So I told them a lie, that my mother was sick (she was not, and in any case she was in Italy), which they accepted without question. I had lasted almost a month.

I think that my bosses, like all the English lower classes and the poor, subsisted largely on fish and chips for their dinners and high teas for supper. The fish and chips were fetched when needed by anybody who happened to be around. The grubby fish and chips shop was about a block of dilapidated one-family dwellings away. It consisted of a counter behind which there was a large caldron of hot, nasty, smelly fat in which the fish and the potatoes were fried. Both the slabs of amorphous white fish—cod, I think—and the cut-up potatoes were kept on a nearby stand and replenished several times a day. The owner and his wife, grubby like the shop, did the cutting up of the fish and chips, and they also did the frying. If one was lucky, the food was fried freshly when purchased, but most of the time the fried fish and chips were kept warm in a large pot placed near the gas range that held the caldron filled with the cooking fat. On the counter there was a pile of old newspapers in which to wrap the fish and chips, as well as a large bottle of purple vinegar to sprinkle over the food before it was wrapped up. (I could never understand why so many English people said that, to be authentic, fish and chips had to be wrapped in newspaper and sprinkled with vinegar.)

The high tea suppers, on the other hand, were strictly home-made. They consisted of fried eggs, fried bacon, fried tomatoes, and fried bread. Like the fish and chips, the whole meal was washed down with strong, heavily sugared, milky black tea.

There were no set times for meals. Hunger alone would drive my boss to send out for the fish and chips or to go into the grubby kitchen to do a fry-up, as the high tea was called. In between meals, we ate, like all the lower classes, stodgy white bread with margarine and cheap jam, washed down again with tea. When my boss was in a sunny mood, he splurged on a pound or so of sweet biscuits, little horrors stuck together with sickly sweet white or pink paste or with some nasty kind of thick jam, which was supposedly made of strawberries or raspberries, but had no taste resemblance to either of these two fruits.

Perhaps I am maligning the diet of the English lower classes of the time, but the food of the people I lived among taught me better than anything in the world the class difference in English life. In Italy, where I came from, everybody ate basically the same things, though the better-off ate more than the poor. Not so in England, where the nonpoor ate a lot of meat and even some vegetables and fruit, cooked in kitchens light-years from the shambled premises of the poor. How well I remember being pitied by my London friends for eating so badly. But though they pitied me, my friends did not feel for the people who ate so badly all their lives. What struck me most was that the English lower classes appeared to be perfectly content with their diet of fried foods, starches, and sugar. The people I knew in Clerkenwell were a cheerful lot who had no quarrel with their status in life. They all paid only lip service to the tenets of the Labour party. I vainly searched for discontent among them and for people who actually would do something to bring about a change for the better.

I managed to get by in London also with the enormous help of Norman Ewer, who was known universally as "Trilby." This immensely kind man was the big-shot editor at the *Daily Herald*, a now defunct London newspaper. Trilby was very amusing and very popular; he admired my lack of fussiness when it came to doing odd jobs, and he insisted on publishing in his paper my little adventures under my name, though he had written them up. He caused me to sell flowers in Piccadilly Circus; those were the days when flowers were still sold there by the "flower girls," actually elderly matrons with a sharp eye and a sharp wit. He also got me work in the kitchen of a stockbroker's family, where it was my task to wash up their breakfast dishes, cloggy with coagulated egg. Once, when I had no money left and was about to be evicted from my cheap, by-the-week bed-sitter in darkest Soho, this immensely generous man gave me one of his blank checks to fill out for whatever money I needed. Fortunately, it was little. I also owe to Trilby Ewer the perfect put-down of a rude person. It is simple, and consists of asking the offender if he or she does not find that his or her manners are a serious handicap in life. Try it, it works.

One of the things I shall always thank Trilby Ewer for was knowing when to buy me dinner. I never said a word about my precarious financial status to him, but he would always find me at the right moment and invite me for a good meal in a good restaurant, which, more often than not, was also a fashionable eating place. I lived in shabby rooms near the LSE, for which I usually paid a guinea, that is, one pound and one shilling a week. (Now, nobody in England reckons money in guineas, which are no longer a legal currency term.) I changed my bed-sitters quite often, when one or another student told me that he knew of a better deal for me. Some of my landladies were clean, others were not, but they all were poor, downtrodden women trying to make a penny as best as they could. Most of the time the toilet was down the hall, as was the bathroom, whose tub usually needed a good cleanup by me before I threw a sixpence into the meter that regulated the hot water dispenser. Sixpence, in a coin, gave me several inches of very hot water, and it was considered good value for the amount of money a bath cost. My landladies never ceased to wonder at the frequency with which I used to have a hot bath.

The furnishings of a cheap bed-sitter are best ignored, except for the gas fire that was to be found in every one of the rented rooms. This fire was started by throwing as many pennies (big copper coins in England at that time) as one could afford into a meter. The gas fires were small and did not heat a room well even when several pennies had gone into activating one. I remember sitting as near as I could without burning up, near such a puny source of heat, trying to get warm and to think how I could improve my financial situation. Somehow, Trilby Ewer always knew when I was getting quite desperate. A telephone call from him and I was off to eating something other than the cheapest bread and cheese. In those days, I used to have one good suit to wear to an "occasion," and every landlady I had was sure to tell me to save this suit for occasions, and to beam at me when she saw me wearing it on the way out of the house. Somehow, the landladies always knew everything about their tenants; like friendly animals of prey, they pounced out of their dark rooms (invariably situated next to the front door) to keep track of their tenants' comings and goings.

Decently dressed, I went to meet Trilby Ewer, alone or with several of his friends, at such posh places as Simpson's, Wheeler's, the Hungaria, the Savoy Grill, the Café Royal, Quaglino's, and other famous London eating places. I felt much more at home there than in my miserable rooms. Trilby and his friends, and the waiters as well, were showing me the delights of good English roasts and puddings at Simpson's and Wheeler's, the delights of paprika and sour cream in the Hungarian dishes of the Hungaria (where we ate to the sad wailing of violins of the gypsy band), the elegant restaurant cuisine of the Savoy Grill (how I sigh for those unbelievably good grilled Dover soles), the Frenchified adaptations of English home cooking at the Café Royal, and the wonderful, elegant Italian food of Quaglino's. This largess was bestowed on me out of nothing but kindness.

Before we married in March 1931, Anthony Standen and I had established that we were in love. He used to come down from Billingham, the ICI plant in County Durham where he worked, to see me for weekends, or I went up there to see him. I used to take the midnight express train to Edinburgh from St. Pancras Station, which in those days was not considered a quaint monument, but an elderly railway station. Around four in the morning I had to change trains in Darlington to a local line that went to Stockton-on-Tees, the nearest railroad station to Billingham. Darlington was not only an important railway junction, but also the place from where England's first train had run to Stockton-on-Tees. In memory of that historic event, the first English locomotive was kept as a giant souvenir in Darlington station. I remember inspecting it in the early dark and dusty dawn of England's industrial north and having a cup of grisly tea in the all-night station restaurant. Once in Stockton, the problem was to get to Billingham, about three miles away. Usually, the night police patrol car was at the station, waiting for an opportunity to put down crime. It was always easy to persuade the bored cops to give one a ride to Billingham. If no ride was available, I simply waited for the first bus, which came around 6:30 and got to Billingham in about an hour's time, as the bus meandered all over creation. Since one or the other of the two of us was going up north or coming down to London every weekend, Anthony and I became well known to the train personnel. The ultimate triumph was to be allowed to ride from Stockton to Darlington or vice versa on the engine, to watch the fireman put coal on the locomotive's fire, and to buy the driver a cuppa in return for his hospitality.

It was no problem to arrive early in Billingham, where Anthony's landlady was expecting me for a breakfast of bacon, fried eggs, fried tomatoes, and fried bread, with the obligatory black, sweet, milky tea. This was the standard fare of the English working classes, and good eating if the frying was done carefully in fresh, clean fat. Since Anthony's landlady was a house-and-kitchen-proud English north country woman, her breakfasts were something I looked forward to when I went north. But what on earth does one do in a city like London so early in the morning? I can't remember how or why we thought that Dean's Yard in Westminster would be a good place to spend early morning hours. But there we were, inspecting every detail of the place, and I am ashamed to say, hiding or changing some of the milk bottles an early dairy delivery had left at the door of the deans of Dean's Yard. Mercifully, we never found out

what the worthy householders said when they either did not see
the milk on their doorsteps in the usual manner, or when they
found the wrong amounts of either too little or too much milk
or cream.

Recently, I reread the two authors that best capture the feeling
of Berlin life in the twenties and thirties, namely, Christopher
Isherwood and Harry Graf Kessler. Isherwood's books *The Last
of Mr. Norris, Prater Violet,* and *Goodbye to Berlin* are known in
America thanks to *Cabaret,* the superb play and movie they
inspired, which made Liza Minnelli and Joel Grey famous. I
cannot think of any other play or novel that captured the essence
of a certain city and a certain time in its history as well, and that
made such an indelible impression on the public at large as did
Cabaret. Harry Kessler's diaries, translated into English from
their original German, were published in this country by Holt
in 1971, under the title *In the Twenties* (though they cover the
years 1918 to 1937); they are not well known even to American
historians. Unfortunately so, since Kessler knew everybody and
had been everywhere, from the 1918 Armistice between Germany and the Entente, as the Allies were then called, to 1937,
when Hitler had made it imperative for him to flee Germany.

Berlin was unquestionably the most intoxicating, scintillat-
ing, and unusual city in Europe at the time. Even I, who did not
live there, could not escape the lure of the place. Whenever I
had the money, earned at some indifferent London job, I went
to Berlin to look for some excitement. I went there many times,
but, unfortunately, I am now unable to date what happened
when.

I recall visiting my father in Berlin's foreign office, the *Auswärtiges Amt,* known as the AA, on one of his periodic visits to
Berlin. At the time, I greatly admired Isadora Duncan's appearance and tried to dress like her, in a flowing, loose, puce-colored
garment, with my longish blond hair held back by a satiny
headband. My father took one look at me, and went to the door

to see if the passage to his office was empty. It was. Not wasting time with explanations, he took me through a number of staircases to the back entrance of the AA, set me in the street, and told me, fury in his voice, never, but never, again to sully his eyes, his office, and the whole German Foreign Office with the getup I was wearing. I was very surprised because I thought I looked charming and because, until that day, my father had never lost his temper with me.

Though I knew, personally or by hearsay, most of the politicians of the time, the group I traveled with was very different from that associated with my father and my relatives.

In a way, provided one's politics were not right of center, everybody knew or had at least heard of anybody else in Berlin. My father's friends and acquaintances were the now-staid fathers of the Weimar Republic, but the circles I frequented on my sporadic short-term Berlin visits were composed of theatrical or literary people. I lived in cheap rented rooms; my landladies were harmless middle-class women who sighed for the dear departed kaiser and who would have taken a dim view of me had they not needed my rent money. Knowing French and English, I had no trouble finding little, inconsequential jobs; I typed envelopes, translated and wrote letters for commercial gents, and worked as a salesgirl in a department store, selling to clients who did not speak German.

My Berlin was a circle of overlapping social circles. My father's friends and the people I had been friendly with in Geneva had introduced me to some very rich Jewish intellectual businessmen, who were Berlin society and who financed left-wing causes. I remember going to tea at the house of one such man who lived in the smart Tiergarten Viertel in a house sumptuous with rich hangings and antiques. He lived with his mother, an elegant and forceful matriarch who sat enthroned in a Jacobean chair while she poured out the tea from an English silver tea trolley. After passing her dispassionate eyes over me, she knew that I was harmless. Indeed, nothing could have been further from my mind than to be after her very eligible only son, who had brought me to his mother's house to prove that Berlin department store owners did have intellectual interests.

Brecht was a great friend of mine, and I never knew that he was not the most considerate and kindest of men. He was always very concerned about my health; once, when I had the sniffles, Brecht insisted on taking me to see his friend, the very well-known Dr. Sauerbruch. I knew this medical man was professionally millions of light-years above sniffles, but since Brecht insisted on his seeing me, he did so, letting me go with a friendly pat on my behind and a prescription for a cold remedy. At the time, Brecht was still quite flush with the success of his *Threepenny Opera,* which had run for a seemingly endless number of performances. I knew it well, and I still have in my possession the first German records of the work, with the original performers. I have always thought, and still think, that no other play or music, other than first-class achievements, is as typical of the Berlin late twenties. (*Die Dreigroschenoper* was first performed in Berlin in 1928.) Through Brecht, I met his friend Piscator, who had staged *The Threepenny Opera* and most of Berlin's incredibly avant-garde plays. Piscator had a kind of doomed appearance, which he emphasized with a doomed tone of voice. Gloomily, he once told me that he planned to stage all of Shakespeare's dramas if he could find the proper actors. This struck me as strange; if there ever was a theater-conscious town, it was Berlin, where actors did quite well compared to the rest of the population.

In the Berlin I knew, there was, on the one hand, poverty of the most abysmal kind and, on the other, gross luxury. Housed inhumanly—to say the least—in Berlin's famed Hungerhöfe, the horrible multiple courtyards of the tenements in the eastern part of the city, men had been unemployed for years. Penniless, and without any hopes, they hung around in the streets. In contrast there were the exquisite villas, sometimes showcases of modern architecture, in Berlin's beautiful suburbs, where forest and multiple lakes met to make the exquisite playgrounds for those who could afford it. Indeed, Berlin was a paradise for people with money, whatever their taste. Prostitutes with high red boots catered to a kinky clientele, as did the transvestites of both sexes. When you walked in westend Berlin, you never knew who would approach you for heaven knows what nefarious ends.

There was one institution in Berlin that had become a symbol for the city. It was the Haus Vaterland, a big building with a series of cafés, each one representing a famous German sight or place. I remember especially the café where an enormous water-fall thundered down on one wall to Wagner's music. I knew the water was real, but I could never find out how it could come down with such a roar without splashing even a drop on the nearby tables. All the big and rather dubious Berlin restaurants and cafés sported table telephones so that you could call up the man or woman who had caught your fancy, and then make a genteel pickup. The clientele of these places usually included both well-dressed ladies and gentlemen and hoods with a few marks in their pockets. Where else would the underworld be so admired by the general public as to have a ball of its own? I remember the newspapers running pictures of the underworld hoods, all formally dressed in tuxedoes or even in tails, and their girls, dripping with probably stolen jewels and lace. How could the city's frenzy be anything but self-destroying and come to its bitter end when Hitler came to power?

I knew I wanted to have nothing to do with Germany very soon after I went to Berlin in the spring of 1933. I was hanging around London, when a now defunct magazine and the *Yorkshire Post*, a newspaper, proposed that I should go and write firsthand reports on the Nazi power struggle. I cannot remember how I heard that a room was going cheaply in a *pension* on the Nollendorfstrasse, a convenient location for a reporter since it was central, with excellent communications to every part of the city. So I settled in a nice room, with an agreeable landlord who did not mind my coming and going at all hours. I congratulated myself on having found such peachy surroundings, but not for long. After having supper with my relatives on my first Berlin day, I turned up around nine o'clock in the evening at the Taverne, a beer restaurant that had become the meeting place for American and English journalists. Since I had an English name, lived in England, and was writing for the British press, the Taverne was the place for me to be, I had been told in London. The assembled company of journalists and their friends made me immediately welcome, and I, full of pride and joy, told about my pleasant new room. A general hoot of laughter went up, and I was informed that I had settled in one of the best-known neighborhood brothels, in the very room where Stephen Spender had lived with one of his friends. I burst into tears, and Roger Sessions, the famous American composer, took pity on me. He accompanied me to the *pension*, and told the owner that I was leaving the place right then and there, at eleven o'clock at night. I was told to pack my belongings while he, Sessions, was telephoning a respectable, inexpensive hotel. While I was packing, the owner congratulated me on having found such a fine protector in a few hours, and offered his free hospitality any time I wanted it. That was the last time I laughed in Berlin.

To this day, I cannot speak of Berlin without crying. I was one of the Anglo crowd, which included people who became personal friends, such as Edgar Mowrer, Knickerbocker of the Hearst papers, and Darsie Gillie of the London *Morning Post.* We all knew and reported constantly on the Nazis and on the Jewish persecutions that were becoming worse every day. We knew that you could not pass a certain building in a certain street without hearing the agonized cries of those unfortunates who were being tortured by the Gestapo day and night. Dorothy Thompson came, and I did some work for her since she did not know German. All of us knew what was happening in Germany, but nobody in America or in England believed our stories, or they did not want to believe them.

7. NEW YORK

*R*oger Sessions and his then wife, Barbara, had become firm personal friends, and he left Berlin at the time I did, he for the United States and I for London. He had promised to find me a job in America when he got home, because I had to be able to support myself wherever I was. About six months later, a cable from *Fortune* magazine arrived, offering me a temporary job checking one of their foreign stories for accuracy. I had never heard of the magazine, and I remember asking various London journalist friends if I should take the offer. I did take it, phoned my parents in Milan that I was leaving for New York, borrowed money for my passage, and arrived in New York very late one Tuesday night. I spent the remainder of the night in a hotel on Lexington Avenue, near the Chrysler Building, where *Fortune*'s editorial offices were located on the fifty-second floor. From that floor, I had my first view of New York. I found out that I owed my good fortune to Roger Sessions, who had prevailed on Archie MacLeish, then a *Fortune* writer, to hire me for four weeks at a salary of $27.50 a week (when the dollar was still worth a dollar).

Fortune had been founded in 1930 by Henry Luce to inform the literate American public about big business. Luce, who had invented *Time,* a weekly newsmagazine, in 1923, felt that the great American public was ignorant about the role and the activities of America's big corporations. The new magazine was meant to, and did, shed a careful, sharp light on the nation's biggest establishments. Besides big business, *Fortune* also investigated foreign affairs; one issue was devoted to Italy, and I was hired to check it for accuracy. (It had been realized that only a person fluent in Italian and acquainted with Italian affairs could do the job; I fit the role, and hence I was hired to do the job.) The magazine was splendid beyond belief, big in format, handsomely printed on fine paper, and filled with lavish photographic illustrations of the articles. I had never seen such a magazine before; further, I never even thought that such a thing could exist, even in America. I suspect that my feeling of awe and wonder was also held by the general public. *Fortune* was a commercial success as well as a triumph of mind over matter, expressed by the willingness with which most corporations consented to be helpful to it. Aside from big corporations, the magazine also investigated such cultural American phenomena as the Nervous Breakdown and College Education, and political institutions like the Chicago Democratic party.

Fortune Editorial operated on a system which, I believe, had been invented for Mr. Luce's successful newsmagazine. The staff consisted of the editor, the writers, and the researchers. The first two were always men and the researchers had to be intelligent young females who had accepted the fact that they would never, in those days, become *Fortune* writers, no matter how capable they were. The researchers assembled an extremely large amount of information on a given subject, enough to make a book of it, by scrutinizing anything that had ever been written about it. Researchers went out of town as a matter of course, to investigate on the spot and to interview people who might be for or against the researcher's subject. Then they presented the voluminous material to the man who was to write the article. He then assimilated all the research, and decided if he had all the information necessary for his job. Usually, he decided to do some interviewing himself, contacting the top people in a corporation, for instance. (I was always surprised with what willingness the bosses and VIPs consented to a *Fortune* interview, which basically came down to a drilling, no matter how fair we all tried to be.) The written story then went to the editor for final approval and also back to the researcher, who checked it word by word for sense and for accuracy. This was done by placing dots over each word to show that the checking had been done properly. The checking system worked so successfully that I believe it is used to this day, a lifetime later, on *Time* magazine.

I was quickly initiated into the *Fortune* fact-checking system, since I started working immediately the morning after my arrival, when I saw New York City for the first time from high up in the Chrysler Building and thought how much the city looked like its photographs. After a short introduction to the editor, a young woman who identified herself as the head of the researchers led me to an empty desk in a large room where a dozen or so young women sat at desks heaped with papers. She explained the *Fortune* checking system to me and told me to work immediately on the Italian issue. (I am sorry to say, I do not remember a thing about that one-nation issue.)

In those early days, the magazine was run informally. Writers and researchers were personal friends who saw each other socially. As friendly as we were personally, the writers and researchers fought an unending battle over the work. The writers complained that the researchers were both picky and uppity in questioning their facts. The researchers complained that the writers were shiftless, leaving their writing until the last moment, when it could not be properly checked, and embroidering their stories with a lot of stuff that they had dreamt up themselves. When business relations became too acrimonious (though they never seemed to interfere with social relations between writers and their researchers), the matter was brought for decision to the editor. Occasionally it would happen that the researcher was not satisfied with the editor's verdict. If she felt strongly enough about the matter, she could go to "Our Founder," the Boss of all Bosses, to Mr. Luce himself, and have him decide the matter. Mr. Luce was always available to a *Fortune* researcher and, as I know from experience, he listened most carefully to what we had to say. Then he settled the matter, sometimes finding for the researcher, sometimes for the writer. There never was the slightest doubt in our minds that he settled the right way. I have never encountered any other organization where the top boss could be seen by a lesser employee as a matter of course.

Mr. Luce had just married Clare Boothe Brokaw. From their holiday—in Cuba—Mrs. Luce brought each of us researchers a bottle of perfume; mine was a beautiful jasmine. We debated whether we should thank her jointly, but finally decided on individual letters.

I shall always remember with gratitude how kind *Fortune* and its people were to me, an extremely European young woman. Not knowing anybody in New York, I made all my friends through the magazine. Office life was informal. I remember seeing on the bulletin board a pathetic notice from Mr. Luce himself asking that the writers wear matching suits and real shoes, rather than dirty old jackets and sneakers, when they went to interview the tycoons they had to write about. I was friendly with everybody, enjoying particularly the freedom and the absence of politics in the office. Only recently, when I read about the early days of the magazine when I was a part of it, did I discover that there were great struggles going on among Mr. Luce, some of his editors, and some of his writers. This discovery came as a total surprise to me, making me wonder if I was so taken up with having a foothold in the United States at last that I did not notice what went on around me.

Though *Time* was the older, perhaps the flagship magazine,

Time and *Fortune* had nothing to do with each other, at least as far as the work was concerned. Both magazines were kept strictly apart by Mr. Luce, and had nothing in common. Each magazine had its own staff and its own offices; *Time*'s offices were located on a different floor of the Chrysler Building, before moving some years later to its own building in Rockefeller Center. We *Fortune* people, who produced such a spectacular magazine every month, considered ourselves vastly superior to a lesser and weekly publication like *Time*. Why there was such distance between the two periodicals, children of the same father, I cannot say, though I imagine that Mr. Luce wanted and kept it that way.

Some writers and researchers became very good friends of mine, and I always thought well of the various editors who were my bosses at one time or another. Eric Hodgins, who wrote the charming *Mr. Blandings Builds His Dream House,* was a most understanding man who cheered me up no end one day. Due to my poor checking or to a printer's error, several zeroes had been left out in an important figure in an important article. Naturally, complaints began to stream in, which I, as the article's researcher, had to answer; researchers always had to deal with complaints. Not knowing what to say, I asked Eric Hodgins' advice. He listened carefully and then laughed out loud, telling me that when a magazine printed as many figures as *Fortune,* errors were bound to happen. I seldom have felt as relieved at my boss's attitude, having been certain to get a good chewing out, at the very least. Mr. Ingersoll, who also served as one of the frequently changing editors of the magazine, was also a trifle eccentric. He used to have an ants' palace in his office, for educational purposes, and he also liked to sit in the nude in those days before air conditioning. From my nearby desk, I routinely saw people open his office door and then, after a startled glance, hurriedly slam it shut.

Once my entire New York life was tied up with the magazine, it was only natural that my intimate friends were chosen among the writers and researchers. My specific friends were Dwight Macdonald, Jim Agee, and Ed Kennedy. Ed was a funny little man who had written up the eternal conflict between writers and researchers as a *Fortune* story. This story was widely circulated on the magazine, and also given to Mr. Luce, who chuckled when he read it. The thesis of the story was that writers and researchers were, by the nature of things, natural enemies and that it was futile to expect any other but a battling working relation between them. I fully agreed with Ed Kennedy, and as things go, I found that the "natural enemy" theory applied to other endeavors, such as the relations between editors and writers of books.

Dwight Macdonald was incredibly kind to me in my early *Fortune* days. He made it possible for me to open a bank account by lending me the money needed for a reserve. My bank account, impossible without his help, proved to be a godsend as I was learning the American credit system, that is, paying bills by check. I remember how proudly I drew a check for twelve dollars to pay the weekly rent on my furnished room on West Twelfth Street, and how proud I felt when I deposited my, by now, increased salary check in the bank. Dwight generously took me to be introduced to his fiancée, Nancy Rodman, who remains a close friend of mine to this day. Dwight came originally from Chicago, I believe. Even before he left *Fortune*, he was mostly interested in politics. I, at that time, could not muster the slightest interest in American affairs. Dwight could not understand my lack of interest, and I was never able to explain to him why I was so taken up with my work and with adjusting to a new way of life. I was his researcher on an article on the "nervous breakdown," which took me to every doctor and every establishment between Washington and Boston that had ever dealt with a nervous disease. What I will always remember about the subject is that even sane people must have had periods of insanity when their lives got too complicated. The thin and often invisible line dividing sanity from insanity became very clear to me when I visited St. Elizabeth's Hospital for the Insane in Washington. I was full of this sad truth, and I could talk to Dwight about nothing else for a long time. Dwight retaliated by telling me all about American left- and right-wing politics and politicians, which bored me to no end. (I think that until after the Second World War, Europeans were as ignorant about the variety of American politics as the Americans were of European ones.)

I saw a good deal of Dwight and Nancy, who had been married by then, in their own home. They were sociable people, and so were their friends, New York's liberal and left-wing intelligentsia, whose names did not mean anything to me then, but whose importance in shaping the climate of the times I recognize now. The one person I can still see is Mary McCarthy, holding forth over a group of men; she was a pretty young woman who talked and talked and talked, and who reminded me of a provincial muse. As far as the political talk among Dwight and friends went, I felt superior and repulsed at the way these well-bred, well-dressed people would spout verities when they had never known what living in a dictatorship was like. But Dwight and Nancy Macdonald, I thought then, as I do now, did many more good works than anybody I had ever known.

Jim Agee became my confidant in spiritual and temporal matters. When I first met him, his salary was even lower than mine, though I am happy to say we were both given raises soon after. (His raise, he being a man and a writer, was much higher than mine; but neither I nor anybody else questioned this.) Jim was battling Mr. Luce at that time, because Mr. Luce wanted Jim to go to the Harvard Business School since he considered him (as did everybody else) a fine writer. Jim won the battle, and became more and more interested in his own writings. A turning point in his life had been a *Fortune* trip he took with Walker Evans, the great photographer, to do a story on the rural South. There he saw what poverty really was like, he said, adding that he felt ashamed to interview those poor rural blacks in their decrepit hovels. Jim was still married to his first wife, a conventional-looking woman who was angelic in putting up with her husband's female friends. Jim liked women, with and without sexual dalliance, the way he liked to drink sloe-gin fizzes. I remember sitting in a neighborhood bar with Jim. We were baring our lives to each other, and drinking sloe-gin fizzes. How American I felt, sitting in a bar with an American man and an American drink! I never kept in touch with Agee when we were both no longer with *Fortune.* But all my long life I have been friends with Nancy Rodman Macdonald, even when she divorced Dwight.

Thanks to my background and my ignorance of American business, I became a cultural researcher for *Fortune.* Researchers were given ample scope to assemble the facts and to check them when the story had been written. We had good travel allowances, and a free hand with our daily expenses. The most glorious research I ever did was for John Chamberlain on the Chicago Democratic party; I was given money with which to bribe parties opposing the machine to give us their views of what was going on. John, his wife, and I traveled to Chicago by car for the final interviews. On the way we visited the Gettysburg battlefields, lying hot under the August sun, and the home of Warren G. Harding in Marion, Ohio. It was a great trip. It was also a memorable trip because the Chicago Democratic party did a lot to open my eyes to the daily facts of American life. I remember putting my fingers into the fissures of a badly constructed wall in the Chicago stadium to be able to say that the building was shoddily built, and I remember going around with the story's photographer to see the illegal betting sheets put up in the back of some little, legal, but very shady enterprise. I remember putting money into the closed umbrella (which makes a wonderfully casual receptacle for illegal funds) of Umbrella Sam, a famous figure of the time who worked for the city machine *Fortune* was investigating; and analyzing the exact racial composition of Chicago, down to the one lone Persian inhabitant who tended the baths. I researched the article in Chicago for several months, and went back to check it on the spot. John Chamberlain, the most wonderfully kind, intelligent, and saintlike man I've ever known, told in his book about the shocked silence when I opened the interview with Mayor Kelly, the boss of the Chicago Democratic party, by asking him how he made his money. I can't remember what he told me, but finding out how somebody makes his dough still strikes me as being the main thing all Americans want to know about each other.

I imagine that some writers had favorite researchers; some even married them. If there was any canoodling going on, I did not know or care about it. I was fully occupied, privately grieving over my own unfortunate marriage (I am glad to say I seldom talked about it). Being a cultural researcher, I never did work on corporation stories with the glamour writers such as Charlie Murphy, Green Payton, and Charles Wertenbaker. But everybody, as I said, was on amiable terms with one another. I had a heavy pink silk kimono, lined gloriously with more heavy red silk, which a writer (I don't remember who it was) brought me back from a Japanese business trip. I remember being taught, by some not-remembered writer, how to drop camphor balls out of the fifty-second-floor office window to the pavement below. Spitballs could do as office ammunition, but only, and I stress only, camphor balls would be used for our nefarious sport because only camphor balls would disintegrate on their long trip down, and not hurt any innocent passerby. However, after a considerable time, there were armed (I was told) FBI men keeping *Fortune* under observation from the rooms of nearby buildings.

Though the problem of anti-Semitism was never mentioned at *Fortune,* I realized that it existed in the United States. I must have interviewed somebody connected with the Schwab banking family who told me that in spite of his position as one of America's most prominent men, and in spite of his numerous charities, Mr. Schwab had not been admitted by some men's club because of his race. I remember breaking out into tears when I heard that Americans could be so prejudiced. But Louis

Kronenberger, an extremely intelligent and talented young man, who later became one of America's better-known writers, must have been touched by my reaction. He told me that up to the age of twelve, when he left his native Cincinnati, he was totally unconscious of any anti-Semitism. His family had been a prominent one, and so well known for being sociable that it was extraordinary for him to realize that it was disadvantageous to be a Jew. I am sure that Louis Kronenberger had a great deal to do with my lifelong liking of Midwesterners, whom I still consider freer of prejudices than Easterners or Westerners.

I do not think that writers and researchers remained on those intimate terms after the whole Time, Inc., shop was unionized by the Newspaper Guild. Of necessity, writers became much more punctual with their stories. No longer did researchers do their last-minute checking right in the printing plant, grabbing the galleys as they came off the presses and engaging in spirited arguments with the printers over changes that were necessary for the article's accuracy and the magazine's greater honor. Many are the times when I saw the sun rise over New Jersey, where *Fortune* was printed in those days. But neither I nor any of the other researchers ever complained about the overtime we had to put in because of our late story writers, since after any such bout we were given, without a murmur, several days off to recuperate from our fatigue. All this stopped, so I was told, when the writers were made to pay out of their salaries for the researchers' overtime.

The researchers, my colleagues, could not have been nicer to me. On paydays, we lunched at the old Murray Hill Hotel, which had a bird cage in the middle of the lobby and which made the most divine corned-beef hash I've ever eaten. I think still of Millie Schwarz with great affection. Millie invited me to her elegant home in Greenwich, Connecticut, where for the first time I realized that trees and lawns, not only skyscrapers, grew in America. Even to this day, most Europeans are very surprised on finding that there is an enormous amount of open countryside in the United States. I still cannot go anywhere in America without thinking of what countries poor in arable land, like China and Japan, would make of the land Americans do not consider fit to cultivate.

To this day, I am grateful to Florence Horn, who did such a lot to make me acceptable to Americans and to make America acceptable to me. Florence, a small, dark Midwesterner, occupied a position of her own among *Fortune* researchers. She was a kind of fountainhead of researcher wisdom who knew all the ins and outs of the magazine stories and was trusted by everybody in the Luce organization, which, including *Time,* she knew very well. Florence had been to Brazil for *Fortune,* where she befriended an excellent painter of Italian origin, Candido Portinari, and made his work known in the United States. She was wise enough to recognize my abysmal ignorance about how to dress properly when I went out for the magazine; in short, she was good enough to tell me how to behave properly in New York. I was always very happy to know that somebody cared enough to tell me (most discreetly, in order not to hurt my feelings) when and where I should buy myself new dresses (at Lord and Taylor, if anyone really wants to know), to point out what I should order or drink in a restaurant, and how not to attract attention, for Florence was a lady in the old-fashioned sense of the word. She was fond of gardening and of cooking, and she and I spent quite a lot of time in her own small kitchen trying out Italian food, which was new to her. I showed her how to make *soffritto,* the Roman beginning of many dishes, consisting of hot olive oil in which minced parsley, onion, and garlic were cooked. This brought on a great bout of nostalgia for the Rome of my childhood, which in turn prompted a nostalgic conversation about food that went on for hours at different times. I wondered if the food itself or its smells were nostalgia-makers. Even then, nostalgia was not my thing, but I still think that since ducks need a little puddle of water to wallow in, mankind also needs its wallows; nostalgia is one of them. For a cook I think it most rewarding to gratify the culinary nostalgias of one's friends. Discovering them is a lot of fun and brings frequent surprises about personalities as well. One day when discussing food nostalgia, Florence, whose mother was a celebrated home cook of true Americana (biscuits, shortcake, chicken pot pie), declared with great vehemence (surprising, I may add, from this quiet soul) that her food nostalgia consisted of never, but never, having to eat what her mother cooked so well and so willingly. Don't believe for one minute that food nostalgia relates to *good* food! One of my sons feels the keenest nostalgia for the canned ravioli he adored in childhood. To this day, I believe that cooks should cater frequently to the food nostalgias of the people they cook for. Discovering the favorite dishes of somebody's past, and making them, shows, as few gestures will, that one really cares for a person. Lasting friendships are created this way. One such relationship, very dear to me, was cemented with a superior dish of milk toast, which this man had been craving for a long time; even his charming inamorata never suspected this innermost need of the man she loved.

When you cook for somebody's nostalgia, remember that memory in general, and of foods in particular, is not necessarily realistic; the past is often recalled as better or worse than it actually was. To re-create a dish, you must re-create the memory of the dish rather than the authentic recipe. This means trying to find out what element of it triggers the nostalgia; it might be nutmeg or sage, the sweetness of corn, the crispness or mushiness of vegetables, the heat of a curry, the mushrooms in a stew, or what have you. In all such cases, do not follow your own cooking inclinations; remember you are cooking for nostalgia, and the point is not to create a three-star dish, but to make joyful eating for the nostalgic.

Natasha von Hoershelman was another researcher who became a great friend. She was a genuine Russian aristocrat, who with her sister Lola had been brought over to America by one of the American committees that practiced good deeds in Russia just after the Revolution. The two very young girls then finished their education at Wellesley College. Natasha was a blonde, with Russian features, and she looked best in very short, boyish shorts, which she wore when we went to Connecticut for weekends. The New England farmhouse had been rented by Dwight Macdonald, if I remember correctly, and we used it as a country retreat on our Saturday-Sunday free days. On Tuesdays and Wednesdays, the house was used by some *Time* personnel, whose free days, or weekends, were Tuesday through Thursday, since the magazine closed on Monday night. This house-sharing arrangement worked very well, since employees from both magazines were nice people who cared sufficiently for each other to leave the common weekend place neat and tidy for the incoming tenant. All I can remember of Connecticut are the endless walks I took with Natasha through the countryside, to the dismay of Geoffrey Hellmann, a New York writer who belonged to our group. Geoffrey was tall, well-groomed, rich, and laid-back in character. He regularly squired Lola Hoershelman, Natasha's sister, around; she was poor, lively, and exotic, a complete opposite to the conventional Geoffrey. Lola later married Ralph Delahaye Paine, managing editor of *Time,* who was highly regarded by Mr. Luce. She was unimpressed by the honor of being summoned to the Luce plantation in South Carolina. All she said when told by Paine that she had to go, I am told, was, "Now I will have to buy a girdle!"

At the end of the six months allowed me in America, I went back to England to get my permanent visa. I went to London and to Milan without regrets, and my feeling of elation at having a good job in the United States increased with every day I was out of America. My parents were very pleased to see me settled in a place that I loved and admired, as I did New York. There I was making new friends all the time, meeting interesting people, going to Long Island and Connecticut on weekends, to plays and concerts; in short, I was becoming thoroughly acclimated to American life.

I learned more from researching for *Fortune* than from any

other job I have ever held. In fact, I don't think I could do what I do now without that experience. The job eventually became a well-paid one, *Fortune* being one of the rare places where staff got raises without having to push for them—and this in pre-Newspaper Guild days. I still have friends I made in those days, and I still bless Henry Luce.

8. BOSTON, BRAZIL

I was settled in New York, and happy to have the job on *Fortune* magazine. I had met interesting new people and made new friends. Among them were two friends of Jim Agee's from Harvard. Otto Schön René was very handsome and elegant, whereas Franklin Minor was neither. Jim, Otto, Franklin, and I went to lots of events, such as the six day bicycle races at Madison Square Garden, and to the wonderfully well-acted black *Macbeth* in Harlem and the poetry readings by Edith Sitwell, whose doomed tones still ring in my ears as she recited her poem "Black Mrs. Behemoth." There was no hanky-panky among us where I was concerned. My relation, or my nonrelation, with my legal husband bothered me tremendously, and I felt that our marriage had never been given a proper chance. But I could never talk about myself and my troubles, then or now. I do not think that anybody thought of me as a married woman, especially since I was foreign and had been known by one name only. Since I did not seem to care, why should anybody else?

Jim, Otto, Franklin, and I were mad for poetry. We used to

take the Staten Island ferry so we could shout Auden's and Spender's verses over the water. Jim Agee's slim volume *Permit Me Voyage,* which had won the award of being published in the Yale Series of Younger Poets (1934), was on our lips so often that Jim got very irritated with our enthusiasm. We were proud that Archie MacLeish, an established poet, had been Jim's colleague and that he had been the one to help me come to America by getting me a good job.

Being young, the four of us did all the things one did in New York in those days. We met under the clock at the Biltmore Hotel near Grand Central Terminal (both impressed me with their splendor and with the elegant people in them); we went to dance in the Rainbow Room of Rockefeller Center where, for the first time in my life, I saw a revolving dance floor; we went to see the Rockettes at Radio City Music Hall—I could not get over their precision movements; and we admired the valiant contesters of the bicycle races in the old Madison Square Garden. We also went to the theater whenever we could afford the cheap seats. I remember seeing *Tobacco Road* three or four times, watching the different casts. One reason for that was that the role of the old grandmother was the only acting role I ever wanted to play in my whole life (I also never wrote any poetry or wanted to write any). In *Tobacco Road,* the old grandmother ambles to the stage, to moan loudly, without saying a word. I still think that moaning loudly on a stage must be a great deal of fun. I felt I could moan longer and better than any of the actors in the play.

Being young, we loved to eat. I remember the rice and home-made yogurt at a place called the Cedars of Lebanon, and the thick minestrone at the Gran Ticino in Greenwich Village. Jim introduced me to the pleasures of the cheap Childs Cafeteria, with their marvelous butter cakes, a kind of pancake that we doused with thick syrup. Then there was Schrafft's, where I splurged on such weird (to me) concoctions as butterscotch sundaes, consisting of vanilla ice cream thickly strewn with salted almonds, which sat under a river of butterscotch sauce and a

topping of real whipped cream. The menu pointed out that
Schrafft's never used anything but real whipped cream, which
I found surprising since I did not know that whipped cream
could originate from anything other than a cow. I loved going
to the Horn and Hardart Automats, where one dropped a dime
or a quarter into its slot at one of the many little windows among
dozens of similar little windows where a sandwich, a main dish,
a dessert, cake, or pie was displayed behind glass. I was constantly amazed at the big New York cafeterias, where main
dishes were kept hot on steam tables, and the desserts stood
behind glass counters and on the counters themselves. How I
loved those red, red cherry pies, with their cap of artificial
whipped cream (which I learned to distinguish from the natural
product) and, especially, the solid fruit jellies, cut into large
heavy squares studded with raisins and bits of unrecognizable
fruit! When the four of us felt rich, we dined, and I stress *dined,*
at one of the Longchamps restaurants, especially the one in the
Empire State Building. All of us loved the artistic Longchamps
window displays of fresh vegetables; I remember that every one
of them featured a crown of big green peapods. Inside we ate
steak on tables properly covered with white tablecloths and laid
with flatware and nice glasses. At Longchamps, we treated ourselves usually to a bottle of wine, Jim Agee's or my contribution
as the two only steadily employed members of our group; Otto
and Franklin lived rather poorly on little free-lance writing jobs.
The wine was red plonk, being the cheapest on the wine card,
but it did come in a bottle and it had a proper label, which was
enough for us ignoramuses in such matters.

My life was not confined to New York City. I swam in the
Housatonic River in Connecticut where I went to see the Sessions. I even went once to Atlantic City to see the place; what
impressed me was the enormously long wooden boardwalk along
the beach. I went to Boston often; why, I will now explain.
Anthony Standen's mother, a Bostonian named Eleanor Appleton, and even her Boston kin, had *not* disowned me after the
failure of my marriage to Anthony. I imagine that a number of

reasons prompted them to be nice to me; among them was most likely the fact that the poor outcome of our matrimony was not my fault and, also, that I was totally and unquestionably a respectable woman myself, and a pleasant and polite one as well. Greely Curtis, whom I knew from Geneva where he had introduced me to Anthony, remained a staunch friend of mine. He himself had married meantime, and his lovely wife, Liz, became a very good friend as well. When I first knew her, she used to tell me of the famous Boston Waltz Club where the young Boston matrons like herself congregated once a month, I seem to remember, to waltz in the afternoon with Bostonian gentlemen of their circles. Liz owned, from her deceased mother, some lovely old jewelry; I can still see her rummaging through the old pieces and telling me which one of her ancestresses had owned this or that piece. In Boston, too, there was Mrs. Standen's own brother, Uncle (William) Sumner Appleton, who was known for being the founder of the Society for the Preservation of New England Antiquities. The Society preserved fine old houses throughout New England. The headquarters are in the Otis House, a true gem (which was designed by Bulfinch). Uncle Sumner was tall, and quite formal, though always extremely benevolent to young people. He used to lunch with me at the Union Club in Boston where I first sampled and adored forever after that typical New England dish: codfish cakes. To this day, I have never had codfish cakes as light and crisp as those dispensed by ancient waiters, together with a bottle of ketchup. I've made plenty of codfish cakes in my life, but never as good as those in the Boston Union Club! However, the core of Boston's attraction was the three Misses Curtis and their married sister, Mrs. Hopkinson, known as the "Boston Aunts." Strictly speaking, the Boston Aunts were not our proper aunts, but the cousins of my then mother-in-law, Eleanor Appleton.

These ladies were proper Bostonians par excellence and looked exactly the way a proper Bostonian lady did, with thoroughly sensible tweedy clothes, shoes, and hats. They also behaved like proper Bostonian ladies, putting their work (and

work it indeed was) and their inherited wealth to excellent
worthy causes. Aunt Fan had devoted her life to furthering
Chinese cooperatives; Aunt Hat, as dean of a black woman's
college in the South (I think it was the Hampton Institute), had
recognized Dorothy Maynor's voice as a great one and quite as
good as that of Marian Anderson, the wonderful black soprano.
Aunt Peg, the youngest, was the sporting aunt, patroness of the
Myopia Hunt Club and any number of tennis tournaments on
Boston's North Shore. Aunt Eleanor had married Uncle Tom
Hopkinson, a very good painter of official college and corporation heads. This sweetest of all men also painted wonderfully
luminous impressionistic pictures of his five daughters. I remember especially a portrait of three of his girls, which reminded me of the work of Renoir and Mary Cassatt. All the
aunts were extremely kind to us young people, especially to me.
I knew how good they were to me even then, and I hope I
showed my gratitude at the time.

The family fortune, on which Appletons and Curtises lived,
must have been a very considerable one, I think now, though
I never thought about it in one way or the other at the time, any
more than I thought of them as traditional proper Bostonians.
The family fortune came from old Nathan Appleton, who died
in 1861 as Boston's richest man. He had financed textile mills
at Lowell, Waltham, and Lawrence, Massachusetts, and another
in Manchester, New Hampshire. As the tale went, he, a poor
boy, wandering with the usual bundle of his possessions tied to
a stick, came on foot to Boston from New Ipswich, New Hampshire, and made good in the big town. None of his children had
to work when they were grown up; I suspect that, contrary to
the New England work ethos, he considered working for money
not a nice thing for the better classes. And indeed, why should
his children work for money? His daughter Fanny married the
poet Longfellow as his second wife (more about her later), and
the only one of his sons who rose to moderate fame was Thomas
Gold Appleton, remembered mainly (at least in my youth) for
two sayings. One was that "All good Americans, when they die,

go to Paris," and the other and less memorable pronouncement of this stout, elderly *bon vivant,* to judge from his portrait, was calling Nahant, *the* summer resort of proper Bostonians, "Cold Roast Boston."

Considering the number of people who lived on Nathan Appleton's fortune, it must have been a powerful amount of money. But not all of his descendants had been prudent with their wealth. Aunt Fan once told me that my then mother-in-law's father, William Sumner Appleton, senior, was the most disagreeable man she had ever known. He also squandered what money he had that was not tied up in a trust fund on a coin collection that proved worthless, so Aunt Fan said. His family had to go to live in Germany, then a mecca for short-strapped, but trust-secure, Americans, because living there was less expensive than living at home in the United States. Thus it came about that my mother-in-law met Colonel Standen in Germany and married him, a marriage that was to shape my own life many years later.

The unmarried Boston Aunts had two houses, joined together, on the top of Mount Vernon Street. I had been told that they were not designed by Bulfinch, though I had never heard of Bulfinch. This remark did not make any difference to my thinking that the houses were very comfortable. The drawing room struck me as being very much like an English drawing room, that is, a mixture of good old furniture and chintz and beloved little bric-a-brac and unframed photos of classical and other great European sights propped mainly on the mantel, but also on the ancestral portraits and wherever there was any room. Each aunt had a favorite chair, and I was asked not to sit in any of these armchairs. The dining room was large enough to hold two very long tables one Thanksgiving, where one aunt presided over the turkey and another over the ham. What impressed me was the identification of the numerous children of all ages. Each child wore a tag telling his parents, his name, and his age, so that one would know immediately who was who, not an easy thing with some fifty large and small souls eating together on this great American holiday.

Aunt Fan was the oldest of the Boston Aunts and the one who took me under her wing. She was a very energetic lady who, until her death, read and passed on all the mystery and detective stories for the library of the Boston Athenaeum. Like all the Boston Aunts, Aunt Fan was both frugal and generous. Many years later, when Anthony and I were living in Exeter, New Hampshire, a parcel arrived by special delivery at noon on Christmas Day. It contained (a) a half-eaten roast loin of pork, (b) a rather unattractive new purple and white rayon dress from Filene's Basement, (c) a fine big blue and white Canton ware platter, and (d) a pound of S. S. Pierce's best China tea. The note that came with it wished Anthony and me a happy Christmas and also said that since the pork roast had not been eaten the previous day we would be glad to have it, and that the dress was new and would be useful to me since I had so few clothes.

All the Boston Aunts were elderly, or at least well into middle age, and Aunt Fan, as the oldest, presided over the family's summer home in Manchester, on Boston's North Shore, a place that I got to love as much as anybody who ever went there. The house was a big long one, standing on a bluff over the sea. The property was big, reaching to the water, from where we swam across to a forested rock that lay opposite. The wonderful thing about the place was the grounds, which had been left in their natural state of rocks, low huckleberry bushes, and wild grass; only one very small corner had been planted with a lawn and some rosebushes. My memories of Manchester by the Sea center around Aunt Eleanor Hopkinson and her four or five daughters. In the pergola, Aunt Eleanor presided over Sunday lunches, which included her famous peach ice cream. (In the Boston houses of the Aunts, I tasted for the first time in my life that odd Boston specialty, brown ice cream made with Grape-Nuts; the less one says about it, the better.) But Aunt Eleanor Hopkinson was well known for her wonderful food; one of her favorite recipes, which she gave me, was for a savory made with chutney. This kind and generous woman, who also gave me a wonderfully worked silver sauceboat ladle and a pair of grape scissors, was large enough to have her gentle husband, Uncle Tom, tell that on their honeymoon, she was frequently mistaken for his mother. We all adored Aunt Eleanor Hopkinson. One of her daughters was, as many Bostonians told me, the most popular girl in all of Boston, and sought after by dozens of men with marriage intentions. So many of them came to Manchester to woo and to eat and to stay overnight that Mrs. Hopkinson, running out of beds to put up her daughter's swains, simply added a shed to the main house, known as the Bachelors' Dormitory.

Getting out of New York, and especially going to Manchester by the Sea, made an overwhelming impression on me, primarily that America (as I've mentioned before) did not consist only of big cities like New York. Like most Europeans, my visual impressions of the United States came through the movies, and movies showed the big cities like Chicago and Los Angeles as the only places where things happened. (Westerns, with their wide open spaces, were seldom if ever shown in the Europe of my youth.) At the time I also did not realize that most of America lies beyond the Northeast, which I was getting to know. The thought that the United States contained all the nature one could want, and more, bucked me up tremendously and made it even easier for me to settle here.

I was living quite happily in New York, making new friends. One of them was a woman who was perturbed by my nonchalance about my ill-defined marital status, though I was not bothered by it, and few others were either. However, I did think constantly of Anthony, though the pain of it all made it impossible for me to speak about him. My friend was right; a divorce was indicated. I wrote to Anthony for the first time since our marriage five years before (the period we had been apart), and asked him to come to New York on his return to England from Brazil, where his British chemical firm had sent him to fumigate orange trees. Well, Anthony did come, we talked and talked, and after a few days, the inevitable happened. I agreed to go back to England with him. All I remember about that critical time was that I had finished researching for *Fortune* the story of *Reader's Digest.* This article had been a coup for the magazine, because never before had the heads and founders of the *Reader's Digest,* Mr. and Mrs. Wallace, or the editors of their magazine consented to be investigated by anybody in the world. My writer was pleased with my research, and thus I departed for England in the sunniest circumstances possible. *Fortune* was a moral institution, and wife and husband getting back together after many years of separation pleased the editors very much.

Thus I found myself once more in Billingham, in the north of England, to the surprise of many people who knew Anthony as a bachelor. ICI allowed me to go to Brazil with Anthony in the early spring, when he was returning to fumigate orange trees once more. We went across the sea on a freighter that carried a few passengers—and on that trip we were the *only* passengers, apart from a number of bellicose swans destined for Argentina to propagate their species. These large embittered and embattled birds lived in cages on the deck. The midshipmen who looked after them told horrible tales of how the big birds would attack them if they were foolish enough to turn their backs at feeding time. The ship was also transporting several prize Hereford bulls, which lived in an entourage of hay and straw below deck. Once a day, a mild and innocuous bull tender from Hereford would walk his charges on deck, which they did placidly, except when passing by the swans' cages. Then the bulls roared, their keeper shrieked, and the swans made their own horrible squeaking noises.

The captain of the small ship was very pleased to have us aboard. Since he was the captain and since we had nothing else to do on the trip's fortnight, we played Monopoly with him every afternoon and evening, whether he lost or won. The one day we did not play Monopoly in the afternoon, though we did at night, was when Oxford won the boat race against Cambridge. The

captain appeared to be surprised that Anthony, who had gradu-
ated from Oxford with all possible éclat, should care so much
that his university was victorious.

Brazil, to us, meant the interior of the state of São Paolo. It
made me very happy that I would live in a truly Brazilian little
town, because I did not like big cities like Rio de Janeiro. Even
then the industrial capital of the country was São Paolo, but it
was not the enormous city it is now. We stayed in a fancy hotel
for several days. I remember the breakfast waiter peeling an
orange with incredible elegance, round and round, keeping the
peel thin and in one piece before depositing the naked orange
on a large slice of a delicious ripe papaya. I also remember going
to see the opera house, which my grandfather had partly built.
I also went to Butantan, the state snake farm, where poisonous
snakes are milked for their venom to make antisnake medicine.
As it turned out, the captive Butantan snakes were the only
snakes I ever saw in Brazil, save for a listless boa that used to
hang over a brook near the orange groves where Anthony was
fumigating the trees.

The orange trees used to be fumigated to make their fruit
pretty, without blemishes such as the little black spots that
sometimes dot lesser fruit. The fumigation had to take place
only during certain times of the year; why this was so, I never
bothered to find out. But I did know that you can only fumigate
an orange tree when the sun has gone down and before the
heavy nightly dew falls, which means working in the evening.
The weather had to be dry and perfect; as it turned out, Anthony
spent some time waiting for the right weather conditions.

We took a little train to Pitangueira one morning, traveling
through the famous *terra roxa*, red soil country, and passing
enormous coffee plantations on the way. The coffee bushes
stretched into infinity over hill and dale, with *fazendas* (farms)
all sporting a large brick platform on which the coffee beans are
readied for the market. Traveling by train was great fun. I
discovered that, like all passengers, one eats all the time when
traveling. All sorts of food were hawked on the train, as on all

Brazilian trains even now, I am told. Fruits were plentiful, such as bananas, avocados, papayas, custard apples, oranges, pineapples, and even apples, and fresh white cheese resembling a very young Muenster to eat with the fruit, Brazilian style. There was Goyabada, a dense dark-red fruit paste, Brazil's favorite sweetmeat, thin sheets of apricot leather, and half a dozen or so fried pastries. These included *empanadas,* bits of dough stuffed with meat and/or vegetables, banana chips, little sausage rolls; all tasted very good as they emerged from the vendor's metal box, which he kept strapped on his front. Above all, everything tasted freshly made, as the vendor had wrapped his goods in old creased brown paper.

From several phone calls from São Paolo, I knew that we were not staying at the farm whose orange trees Anthony was to fumigate. He had lived there when he was alone in Brazil, but the South African single men who ran the farm for their English landlord could not envision a female sharing their quarters and cramping their style. Considering how these good-looking, charmingly mannered men carried on their bachelor lives, I would have cramped it, most certainly. However, a house had been found for us, a one-story bungalow, in the Rua Amazonas, Pitangueira, Estado de São Paolo, Brazil, to give our full address.

The solid little bungalow in which we lived had a front porch looking out on a painted landscape of steep mountains behind which rose a gigantic yellow moon that twinkled over a silvery waterfall—the whole view a flight of fantasy in that region of thick red earth, coffee trees, and citrus orchards. The house, rented furnished, was sparse and similar to little modern bungalows in the small towns of southern Europe. The parlor, with a parquet floor worthy of the exotic woods of Brazil, had six wicker chairs and one rocker, arranged around a round table covered with a fancy hand-embroidered cloth. An electric bulb dangling from a cord was covered with an equally fancy hand-embroidered lampshade. More hand embroidery lay on the little sideboard. This passion for hand-embroidered objects, common in Latin countries, was the bane of my childhood. I had to learn to make doilies, handkerchiefs, and borders for underwear—the fancier the better. Now, as an antidote to the age of machinery, it is considered more cultural and refined than ever.

The dining room, also parquet, was furnished with another round table surrounded by six straight chairs wearing snow-white cotton slipcovers on their backs, which made them look like spinster ghosts. In view of our temporary stay, this was just the place to eat, but to our friends in the town, a dining room handsomely furnished with preferably large sideboards and much fancy glass and silver on display was the final evidence of respectability.

The dining room led into the kitchen, on either side of which were the bathrooms with a cold shower and several tubs—one for whole immersion, one for feet, and one for hands. Here, the builder had given up plaster ceilings, glass windows, and parquet floors and had reverted to traditional practicality. There were only heavy wooden shutters at the two windows, and all the inside walls stopped about a foot below the ceiling, allowing a flow of cooling air. In the hot parts of Brazil, all the houses used to be built in this fashion. In my travels I stayed in many of these houses (modern ones are like ours), and I found that any suffering from a lack of privacy was amply compensated by the cool breeze and interesting observations on the private habits of one's neighbors.

Our kitchen was even barer and lighter than the rest of the house, with a floor of hard-stamped earth, and shelves on legs standing in empty tin cans filled with insecticide to discourage wandering ants. The stove, typical of rural stoves, was built as an adobe counter along one whole wall, ending in an oven. The iron-topped stove burned a lot of thin, untrimmed tree branches stacked in the pantry. Sometimes, migrations of ants would wander in an aimless manner on the stove, which I doused with an insecticide called Creolina, a name that sounded to me like a beautiful girl's name. No food was ever kept on the stove, and it was thoroughly washed down after cooking. Only the coffee maker stood on it, a tripod just under one foot high. A conical muslin bag held the coffee, through which the water dripped into a blue enameled coffeepot. The system makes excellent, strong coffee, and whenever the muslin bag (washed after each use) looked dim, I bought a new one.

Just as inevitable as the coffee maker in a rural Brazilian kitchen was the water filter—two clay vessels, one on top of the other, where the water passed through a filter, to be drawn from a spigot. It was covered with a chaste white net petticoat, no match for the turreted and painted models of our friends. Since the question of drinking water is one ever present in the minds of Americans, here is what I did and what I do in foreign places: In big cities, like São Paolo or Rome or Helsinki, I drink the tap water. In lesser cities, I ask if the tap water is good and act accordingly. In small Brazilian places, like ours, I drank filtered water. In dubious villages, mineral water. I've always succeeded well with this rule, but others have not always done so I am sorry to say.

The wooden kitchen table also stood in cans of Creolina to prevent encroaching insect life; the Brazilian cockroaches are stupendously big. In fact, anything that held foodstuffs stood in its Creolina-filled cans. All this sounds worse than it was, especially when I think of the cockroaches every New York apartment dweller has to fight constantly and relentlessly.

The kitchen gave into a backyard full of orange trees, one luxurious banana plant, and several mangoes. From the wooden fence that divided us from our neighbors hung long twists of orange peel, drying in the sun, to be used as fragrant kindling. Brazilians, at least in the country, peel their oranges in a single strip, save the peelings, and suck the fruit. I still do the same when I live with a fireplace; the smell from the burning dried orange peel is delicious.

The backyard was inhabited by our chickens, self-supporting like all Brazilian village chickens. They are tall-legged, singularly independent birds, with bare necks and tail ends, close kin to the fighting cocks that provide one of the nation's sports, an illegal one but not less popular for that. As far as I could see, the chickens lived on the orange windfalls and a few handfuls of rice and beans thrown whenever one remembered. Surprisingly, they even laid a few eggs on this diet and made tough, but very flavorful, eating.

Mingling with the chickens like friendly brothers and sisters were half a dozen or so black *urubus,* those domesticated bare-necked vultures, which eat up the rural garbage and everything else scavenger birds will eat. In Brazil they perform such a valuable health service that it is against the law to shoot them. *Urubus* are perfectly harmless and beautiful in flight. My lasting impression of a Brazilian village is a sunlit backyard with dark green orange and mango trees, the ragged, lighter banana shrubs, where chickens and maybe a turkey or two and *urubus* fed together, as well as rows of *urubus* sitting on the kitchen fence as they did in my garden—waiting, waiting.

Our establishment also included a maid, a pretty redhead, aged eighteen, of Italian-born parents, who kept house as she would keep it later for her husband and five children—amiably, willingly, and informally, with bursts of song as she polished the floors and loud screams as she chased the chickens, to seize one for the table. Like myself, she loped around in *tamancos,* high wooden clogs, which had the advantage of keeping one's feet out of the deep red dust or, when it had rained, the deep red mud of the unpaved streets. I still hear our clop, clop, clop echoing in the house. Leonor knew how to cook simple Brazilian food—rice, beans, stews, and rich, eggy cakes. I taught her pasta and sauces, roasts, and cheese soufflés, though most of the time we ate the local diet.

There was no refrigerator or icebox in the house, though this would not be so today. The town's wealthy citizen owned a refrigerator, a status symbol because at that time it was very expensive. Leonor and I shopped daily for food, after my morning coffee and a meticulous toilet, because even in the sticks ladies are supposed to be well groomed as to hair and nails, starched cotton frocks, and for me, shoes, no clogs. The day's meat supply had come earlier, with Leonor. As in the southern Italy of my childhood, one simply bought meat rather than a specific cut of meat, on the principle first come, first served. Not that it mattered much, because all parts of the beef and pork we ate our way through in a year tasted the same. But it was wise to buy the meat early in the day, before it had been set out in the open air, fly bait bar none. Before cooking, the meat was washed in water and vinegar.

The local egg situation was something else, a mystery I never fathomed. What with the poor meat, eggs constituted a welcome change in the diet. Our own chickens were temperamental layers. Either one could buy no eggs from the various ladies who kept chickens, or several dozen at one time, all fresh and obviously newly gathered. With no refrigerator, the eggs had to be used up in a hurry, which is not easy when you take three or four dozen and have only a few in the household to eat them. Never before or since have I had such orgies of sponge and angel cakes, custards and creams. I used to cook straight through all the egg dishes in the *Fanny Farmer Cookbook* I had brought along, and Leonor did her own with her cakes and cookies.

The vegetable and fruit supply came to the house, accepted by me from my rocking chair on the front porch. The marvelous vegetables—cabbages, zucchini, squash, beans, tomatoes— came from a neighboring garden run as a little truck farm by a Japanese family. Everybody worked at it, the smallest of the children weeding with patient, tiny fingers. An incredibly ribald old Brazilian woman provided the salads. She claimed more than twenty children in her day, though we could never pin her down to the names of more than a dozen. The pineapple and avocado man also came by with his mule cart, with very fine fruit, costing a dime or less in those preinflation days. The bread, long Italian loaves, came with the baker's youngest boy, all of five years old.

Everything else we ate and drank, and much of what we needed for daily life, came from Abe's General Store, called *Secos e Molhados,* "Dries and Wets." Just as our town resembled old Western movie towns, Abe's store looked straight out of *High Noon*. It was completely open to the street and sold everything except fresh meat, fresh produce, saddles, yard goods, and furniture. Great sacks of coffee and rice, manioc flour and beans were piled on the floor, with large black coils of chewing tobacco and cartons with hardware, topped by pyramids of the large, coarse straw hats worn by the field hands. Large hunks of dried meat and bundles of salt cod were stacked on barrels of lard, and piles of zinc basins stood on cases of beer, tonic water, gin, and whisky for the nearby English colony of hard-drinking bachelors who ran the orchards fumigated by my husband. Whatever could be hung from a ceiling and from brooms—elastic-sided boots to salami—hung there. The wall shelves were tightly packed with coarse china, pots and pans, fancy cut-glass bowls for wedding presents, and toiletries. You could smell some of the soaps across the store. One whole wall was reserved for the sealed tins of butter from southern Brazil's dairy country, cans of olive oil, vinegars, sauces, and delicacies such as bottled pale asparagus, canned hams, Lipton tea, and English jams. Abe also sold Brazilian wine, good *vin ordinaire* for quaffing, hard candy, and *pinga,* the national strong drink made from sugar cane that is the comfort of the poor. The smell of *pinga* hung over the store; once smelled, it is unforgettable.

Abe was the man who knew everybody and everything, and could fix whatever needed to be fixed. He and his family, who lived in a large house behind the store, became my great friends. They were Greek Orthodox Lebanese—Turks, as the Brazilians called them in their prejudice. The Brazilian Lebanese and Lebanese-descended colony included cotton millionaires and poor backwoods peddlers. Traditionally, the Lebanese were traders of soft goods. Then they changed their peddlers' packs for stores such as Abe's. He had come to Brazil via Canada, where his children had been born and schooled. His brothers, who like him had fled after the Turkish massacres, had lured him to Brazil with tales of gold in the street and with appeals to his family feelings. Finally, he landed in our little town with his wife, his two daughters, and three sons, all married with children when I knew them. He opened his own general store and installed his sons in two others, one a yard goods store and the other a shoe store. Abe and his children spoke English, though Arabic among themselves. But the third generation was truly Brazilian, knowing only Portuguese, the national language. Their house was possibly the finest in town, with a parlor with a great number of embroidered cushions, chairbacks, and curtains, a dining room with a great display of painted china and cut glass, and bedrooms handsome as to furniture and more embroidery. These were the rooms for state occasions, when company came from Rio or São Paolo. Family and guests lived in simpler bedrooms, in the kitchen, and on the porch shady with banana and other shrubs. There I used to sit with the family learning about Brazilian life. In Abe's house I took baths in the real bathtub when the shower at home palled; and when it really mattered that a dish or a dessert be iced, I was allowed to carry it to their house to cool in the big family refrigerator.

We lived Brazilian country-style, and Leonor cooked most of our food because that was the thing for her to do. The basis of a meal, as in the houses of the rich and poor alike, was a large dish of rice and one of black or brown beans. With it, we had two meat dishes, beef or pork, and chicken. With some difficulty, I had to restrain Leonor daily from making more meat dishes, because Brazilians love meat in all forms, and well-to-do families in our hinterland had three, four, and even five meats on the table. We had stewed beef and fried chicken, roast pork, fried pork, and braised pork, in light tomato sauces. We also had potatoes, boiled or hashed or fried; at least two vegetables; a green salad and a tomato salad; and a plate of fried eggs. But I balked at an additional dish of macaroni in a tomato or cream sauce. Everything was substantially cooked in lard and butter and served with a red pepper sauce (optional) that can only be described as being as powerfully overwhelming as tropical nature. The one thing we did not have was *farofa*, a fine powder made from manioc root, a tasteless, pure starch that Brazilians, especially poor ones, sprinkle over all their food the way the Italians sprinkle Parmesan on pasta. I also trained Leonor not to give us *canja*, the ubiquitous Brazilian chicken soup, because I loathe all chicken soups, whatever their nationality. Liquid hen is just too much.

Of course we had dessert. The standard was quince, guava, or banana paste, eaten with a fresh cheese, similar to new Muenster. We also ate cheese with other desserts, with fresh pineapple, with cooked or fried bananas, or with cornstarch pudding, following local fashion. I remember the fresh fruits with great nostalgia. There were bananas, tasting either of apples or peaches, to eat raw (the long green plantains were for cooking), papayas, mangoes, and European-type fruits such as apples, pears, and the most beautiful strawberries.

None of this sounds very exotic, and it wasn't, except for the touches of dousing starch on starch, *farofa* on rice and beans, or frying bananas as a vegetable. Brazil is a melting pot like the United States, with settlers from all parts of Europe, Asia, and the Far East. The part of Brazil we were in was settled by Portuguese and an enormous number of Italians. The settlers there had nothing to do with the plantation and slave economy of the early settlements in the north of the country. Brazil, almost as large as the United States, has the same division between north and south, though the other way around. Our south is kin to Brazil's north, where *Gone with the Wind* was also a best seller. There the food, always on the rice and beans basis, is very different, with strong savory touches of African cooking. In Brazil's south, the food resembles Mediterranean food. Different ethnic groups who settled there contributed Polish, German, Ukranian, and other dishes. Some of the food, such as you find in the fine restaurants of Rio and São Paulo, has evolved into a superb national cuisine, as I found out later. In our part of the country, as described, the food was homey but incredibly abundant. The food on our own table was always sufficient for at least six, though there were only two of us in the household. But people dropped in for the midday meal, which was served

around eleven, following local rural fashion. In Brazil, hospitality is immense. At first, we were formally invited, with much
fuss, and reciprocated. Then we just went and ate with people,
or they came to eat with us, *sans façon*. We had no meal at night
since my husband was away at his work, and I was out visiting
or at home boiling myself an egg.

Anyhow, the food seemed to be gone at the end of the day.
What was left over was collected by a Franciscan monk from a
nearby monastery, who came around in a little mule-driven cart
with large pots. Every day, he made his rounds of the town to
collect surplus food for the poor, of whom there were many.
They lived almost exclusively on rice and beans, prepared with
as much lard as they could afford, doused with manioc flour,
with meat as a treat. Aside from a few leaves of lettuce, they
never ate greens; this terrible diet seemed all the worse considering that we were living in an immensily fertile region where just
a few seeds dropped into the ground would come up with a
bounty. Other than bananas, mangoes, oranges, and a little
lettuce, they hardly ever ate fresh foods.

In everybody's experiences, some stand out boldface. Two
come to my mind when I think of Brazil—first, the hospitality
of the people. About everybody I knew, from well-to-do, to less
well-to-do, to downright poor people, always set the table for
more people than their own family, in case a visitor should drop
in at mealtime. The other is the sight of a waiter in a good
restaurant elegantly peeling an orange.

Brazilian food is extremely varied, reflecting the ethnic back-
grounds of her many settlers: from the Portuguese and the
African slaves who came together, to the Italians and Japanese
in São Paulo, and the Poles and Germans in the south. Aside
from this, there is the influence of French cooking, as in all
civilized nations.

I lived most agreeably in our little house for about eight
months. My days were spent in a ladylike fashion, visiting other
Brazilian ladies in their homes, seeing the Abe family, keeping
Anthony company whenever he was waiting for good fumigating

weather, and learning very quickly and thoroughly that in the Brazil of that time, all women were either respectable or not at all. This was evident when an American friend came from New York to stay with us. She and I took a long trip way into the interior of the country. Our behavior was so dignified, our appearance—in long-sleeved navy dresses—so obviously respectable that we traveled for over a month by bus and on horseback to the Araguaya River, in the deepest interior, without ever arousing even a suspicion of disrespect from the men we dealt with, while the women looked at us unbelievingly and repeated, "What courage, what courage." I rode horseback, wearing the traditional *bombachas*, Zouave-like pants with ornamental stitching up the sides, made by the local dressmaker. But whenever I had to walk through the village on my way back from a ride, I modestly draped a little skirt over my pants.

An old Lebanese taught me how to drive a car on a beach not far from São Paolo, deserted then but now a flourishing resort. On the safe, long beach, he used to crouch on the floor of the car's front, holding down my feet whenever I had to start the car or use the brake. The merry South African bachelors invited me for dinner when they found out that I was friendly with an Englishman who said, often and with emphasis, that no man in West Africa (where he had spent some years) was a man until he had had the clap twelve times. When the time came to go back to England, I wept and wept and wept; I will always feel *saudades do Brasil,* that is, nostalgic for a most wonderful and hospitable country, where I never felt like a stranger.

9. BILLINGHAM, BABY, AND HOME

$\mathcal{B}$ack in the north of England, Anthony and I had to find a house to live in. We both knew that we did not want, under any circumstances, to live in the settlement ICI had put up not far from its plant. The nice, comfortable middle-class houses of the settlement, known as "The Compound," housed most of the nice middle-class chemists employed by the "Works," as ICI was known to its chemist employees. These were subdivided into two classes: people were either organic or inorganic chemists, the first a good thing, the second not (that is how far my knowledge of chemistry went). I must say at once that organic or inorganic, the ICI chemists and their wives were unfailingly nice to me, though they wondered about me, as I found out much later. But their perfect manners, acquired usually from Oxford and Cambridge, made me feel hopeful of my new life.

Through a slow-speaking, slow-moving elderly real estate agent we found a little cottage on Billingham's Church Square, well away from anything that spelled ICI. The little house was one of the cottages in a row that led up to the vicarage, near the church with its Norman tower. The church filled one side of the square, with its building in the middle of the cemetery. Way across from us was a respectable Georgian house, inhabited by the local doctor. At the bottom of Church Square past the main road was a grocery shop, and around the corner from us was a pub and a fish and chips shop. These two were considered amenities by our real estate agent, who praised them with enthusiasm, saying that we could fetch beer any time we wanted and did not have to go out to the pub to drink. Indeed, we fetched beer all the time, in a large white metal can with a hinged lid, originally meant for hot water. We also ate quite a lot of very good fish and chips, which were doused correctly with vinegar and wrapped in many layers of newspaper to keep them hot.

Our house was nice. I liked it very much and resented the attitude of many visitors who said, quite correctly, that it was not a gentleman's residence. It must have been about 150 years old and it was larger than the cottages to either side of it, as my slatternly neighbor told me, whose husband was a parish grave-digger. We got into it by walking seven measured-out steps from the road, through the vestiges of a front garden. In that garden I remember only some giant hollyhocks that grew against the low wall separating our front yard from its neighbors. The living room was on the left as one came in, and quite big. On the right there was a tiny dining room, and on the left a very big kitchen. The floors were flags throughout, and the fireplaces in each room and in the kitchen were the sole source of heating in the house. There were no fireplaces upstairs in the little bedrooms, in the bathroom or in the loo, these being in English fashion two separate entities. Finally, the cold of an English north country winter got to be too much for us, and for the bathroom we bought a small electric heater, to be turned on in times of need.

Cleaning our fireplaces every day, carrying out cinders, and rubbing the whole fireplace daily with stove blackening paste or liquid, is a horrible chore. (No wonder it cured me forever of wanting to have a fireplace for coziness wherever I lived.) Until the advent of a gas poker, I laid the fireplace in the kitchen and living room (and in the dining room if we had guests) in the traditional way, with spills made from old newspapers, a few bites of wood topped with lumps of coal. Local coal was cheap, and we bought it by the ton, storing it in the back under a piece of tarpaulin to keep it from getting wet in the frequent rain. Nobody in England at that time ever dreamt of burning anything but coal. Once, I do not now remember how, we got two old railroad ties, soaked with oil, and sawed them into small pieces. They burned so well, in lieu of spills and wood, that I got a much-wanted gas poker after the ties were burned up. The gas poker was a long piece of iron, riddled with horizontal holes for a gas flame. Eliminating spills and twigs, one put the poker under the coals, lit the gas, and kept the poker burning until the coals were burning properly. The gas poker was my pride and joy, but the men who came to install it did not approve of such newfangled inventions. They told me so plainly, pointing out that none of their wives would ever dream of indulging in such a labor-saving device, their wives not being sissies like some women they could name. In a cowardly manner, I was ashamed of telling the gas men that once, when trying to make a coal fire work in the kitchen fireplace, I had committed the ultimate sin of stimulating the laggardly fire with some shots of kerosene. The fire burned as never before, but it roared up the chimney so violently that all the soot in the chimney was shaken loose, and fell down to extinguish the fire and to blacken walls, ceiling, and every single thing. It took over a week to wash walls and ceilings and to get the soot off everything in the kitchen; the soot, as only greasy soot can, sticks to everything like mad.

Just past the kitchen was the pantry, a very cold place fitted out in the window with a meat safe, which hung out like a wire air conditioner. Bacon flitches hung from the ceiling, along with the long braids of onion and garlic sold at the front door by the non-English-speaking young men from Normandy who came by every two or three months. They always stayed for hours, drinking coffee and beer, because they were happy to be able to talk French. The vicar came by one day, but he left very soon after seeing that our living room was lined with books. Joining our books had indeed produced a formidable array of ancient and modern tomes. Anthony had all the English poets, I had the German and Italian ones, and we used to spend time spouting poetry at each other. We had constant weekend guests who came up from London. I remember one of them, who used to lie in bed all morning, eating chocolates, which struck me as pleasant but abandoned. Though Billingham was surrounded by housing developments for the thousands of workers employed by ICI, we lived in the still intact core of the village as if there were no such thing as a modern chemical industry.

We got out of Billingham very often over the weekend. To Durham, with its marvelous cathedral, all Norman arches and mysterious darkness; to the Pennine mountains in the west, where in a village called Muker I found in the garbage a wonderful old north country cookbook; to the city of Newcastle, where I bought some blue blankets and where we ate winkles from a street stall, using pins to pry them loose from their shells. I remember both of us being driven to London by a friend of Anthony's to see *Snow White and the Seven Dwarfs,* which I thought a very violent movie. We walked over the Yorkshire Dales, to the south of Billingham, eating large farmhouse teas with kippers, fried tomatoes, and prunes with custard. Our lives were pleasant, but always, always, we felt acute nostalgia for the United States.

Like the three sisters in Chekhov's play who sigh for Moscow, we sighed constantly for the United States. There the government did do something to take care of the poor and unemployed (this was the time of Roosevelt's New Deal), but nothing seemed to be done to alleviate the tremendous misery of north England. Wherever we looked and wherever we went away from our sheltered little home, the Depression was raging. Raging is indeed the only word to describe the misery of towns and country around us. North country industrial towns and villages are depressing enough in good times, but then, in the midst of the Great Depression, they looked even darker, damper, and more early nineteenth century than before. Hundreds of out-of-work men of all ages stood around in the streets, and I wished there had been even a little hint of rebellion in the air. But there was none. The men stood around listlessly, like dead birds. I volunteered three days a week in a children's clinic, where one could see their deterioration increasing day after day; I have never gotten over the sight of those starved slum children. Not even in the England of today, prosperous compared to the Depression years, can I ever forget the unemployed.

Meantime, I had become pregnant. I was not feeling very well, so I had pregnancy tests, three of them, done at the University of Edinburgh by way of our local doctor. They had proved negative. In spite of the negative tests, I was indeed pregnant, and finally the doctor said that I had better go home to my parents if anything should go very wrong; as it was, I did not know anybody well enough to ask her to stay with me if I should need help. Thus, in the spring of 1939, we decided to go to my parents in Milan. Unfortunately, Anthony himself was quite ill with a very nasty hepatitis, which enfeebled him to almost total listlessness.

On this first trip back home after settling down in Billingham, I kept on thinking how my interests had changed since my first visit to the United States. Before going to America, politics and more politics had absorbed me completely, in Rome, Milan, Berlin, and Geneva. Now, nothing was further from my mind than the doings of the world beyond my little house. The fact that all my English friends, and especially my husband, cared not one iota for politics had a lot to do with my lack of interest. However, I imagine that, in the last resort, it was I myself who had changed my interest. Never again did politics matter to me, in spite of all the changes in my life.

After taking a look at us and assuring me that my character

and my nature had changed (for better or worse, they did not say), my parents took us to their house in Cerro, a village on Lake Maggiore. There I spent a most wonderful summer, probably the best one of my life. Anthony was recuperating, thanks to injections prescribed by a family doctor, who like so many Latin medicine men believed firmly that injections of various kinds would cure most ills. (I have come to agree with the Latin doctor.)

Cerro is a very small village on the southern shore of the lake; Laveno, to the north of Cerro, is the nearby city you can find on any map. Our house, one of the usual Italian middle-class villas, sat in an enchanting position on a little bluff over the lake surrounded on three sides by trees and bushes where cuckoos and nightingales nested and sang during the spring and summer. The charm of the house went beyond the gorgeous view across the lake to the Monte Rosa and other assorted Alps, whose snows were colored a deep pink by the rising and the setting sun. The garden, or rather an attempted garden, took one down to the seawall. Over the lake on this seawall, leading straight way out into the water, was a big sliding chute. One mounted it on top of the seawall and then chuted straight into Lake Maggiore's tepid waters. On our part of the shore the lake had no beaches and it was very deep right off the shore. The chute slide thus deposited you right into the water; you had to swim once you had slid down. To get out you scrambled up on the shore beyond the seawall. Naturally, the chute was a great local attraction, because there was not a soul in the neighborhood who could not swim; swimming in the lake was one of the reasons Cerro had become a little playground for the Germans in Milan.

Our life was totally painless. The caretaker served as a maid, waiting on us hand and foot. In the evenings, she sat in a corner of the sparsely furnished living room, knitting or mending; one only had to call her name to make her get up with the usual, "Comandi, Signora," to fetch one a handkerchief or whatever. Part of the establishment were two large sheep, Leda and Leandro, which lived in the garden and came when called. They were large, woolly animals; from the top of the head where the wool began to the tail where it ended, each sheep had a neat part through the wool. Thanks to the parting, the sheep looked very tailored, said the *infermiera,* the nurse who came every day on her Vespa moped to inject Anthony. I swam merrily in the lake, since the Italian doctor had said that there was nothing wrong with me but an awful lot wrong with the University of Edinburgh. My condition never bothered me into thinking about it, so that Anthony and I decided to drink systematically all the Italian wines mentioned by Frank Schoonmaker and Tom Marvel in their early book *Come with me through Italy.* We bought the wines locally or in Laveno, and the rarer ones came to Cerro with my parents on weekends from Milan.

We also enjoyed very much the visits of friends from England. I remember best the arrival of two Englishmen who had asked what they could bring to my mother as a hostess present. At that time, decent paper napkins could not be obtained in Italy because they were not made there and not even imported because Italians saw no need for them. My mother, like myself, abhorred the idea of cloth napkins, which came to the table in napkin rings (silver ones if you were *comme il faut*), and were changed once a week. So we asked for the beautiful, thick, large paper napkins that existed in England. Our friends, who drove from England, brought Mama no less than one thousand large, thick paper napkins, tied according to their color into neat bundles. Overjoyed, my mother decided to use the white napkins for our Cerro Sunday dinner. How will I remember my father taking one look at the white expanse of the unfolded paper napkin; he was speechless. Then, still speechless, he got up from the table, took his hat, and left the house. We also were speechless at my father's behavior, so much so that my mother did not move. My father was gone. We found out from the caretaker's wife that he had commanded her husband to drive him to Laveno, from where he caught the train to Milan. He never spoke of the paper napkins when he came back the following weekend, but never again did they serve in lieu of proper napkins when my father had a meal with us.

As I said before, my pregnancy did not bother me at all. Only much later, when my son was several months old, did I know that the fetus does not float freeform in the mother's abdomen, but is properly contained. I wondered what I had done to my poor little boy drinking so much good wine in Cerro and swore to give up even a mild glass of sherry. But the child did not suffer at all from my bibulous ways, and thus I gave up my vow never to touch drink again. We had thought that "Ebenezer," as the unborn was called by us and all people who knew us, would be born on June 12. But June 12 came and went, with no baby in sight. So we took up sweepstakes on Ebenezer's arrival, the winner giving up his money to the newborn. As it was, the child was born only on July 21; I thought that this late date explained why my condition was delicately called an "interesting" one, and gave no more thought to it. However, I was convinced that I would not know what labor pains would be like. I consulted every single female who had had offspring about the nature of the pains, but to no avail. I was annoyed about the whole affair, but there was nothing I could do to learn about it.

One morning late in July, I woke up very early with what I thought were acute hunger pains. Quietly, so not to wake Anthony, I went downstairs into the kitchen and made myself two substantial salami sandwiches. But even after the two big salami sandwiches, I still had pain. Then it occurred to me that my labor had begun. But what to do? A place in a private clinic in Milan had been reserved for me, but how to get to Milan was the question. My mother had gone to one of Switzerland's high mountain resorts to prepare herself for the great event, my father was in Milan, and the only person around was Anthony's sister, a lady who knew art and who had planned to spend the day driving to some ancient church to see its frescoes. For this purpose, she had hired the local taxi driver and his car, and they turned up punctually at the proper time. The caretaker's wife and I, not knowing what stage of giving birth I had reached, decided to send the taxi driver and my sister-in-law to find the local doctor. They came back several hours later, having driven round the countryside asking for the *dottore*, who that day was visiting his distant patients *in situ*. The whole countryside got extremely interested in the Signora Inglese who was also Italian, and helped the search with much goodwill and noise. As I learned later, never before and never after were the country people in Cerro and surroundings so united and anxious to help.

Meantime, at home, I found I had released a lake of water. I was worried, but the caretaker's wife assured me that this was a normal process when giving birth, and she urged me to get interested in a local newspaper. Finally, the *dottore* arrived with my sister-in-law. I was so relieved that I kissed him, though I had never seen the man before. He took one experienced look at me and decided that there was just enough time to get to Milan, if we drove very fast. In no time at all, Anthony, the *dottore*, and I were in the taxi, taking with us a hot water can full of boiled water produced by the caretaker's wife, an old sheet, a pair of scissors, and a *fiasco* of red wine. The trip was a merry one. We drank all the red wine, sang a lot of songs, and trusted God's wisdom. We never needed the boiled water, the sheet, and the scissors (taken along on the principle that one never knew). We arrived in Milan in record time, got to the clinic, and three hours later I delivered our firstborn. My father was out for the day, and he saw me only after the child was born. He was pleased and sent a telegram to my mother in her Alpine resort.

This is not the place to go into the state of Milan's hospitals, suffice it to say that the private Clinica Sant'Ambrogio took good care of me according to their lights. Terrified that I should catch cold, those in charge kept me under three blankets in Milan's summer heat, which is very considerable. To make sure that I stayed well covered at all times, an old nun sat daytime by my side, to be spelled by another old nun at night. For three days after the birth, I was given only coffee and broth, and a good dose of castor oil very early on these days to "clean" me out, as the nun said, holding my nose to make the horrid, viscous liquid go down more easily. The final memory of the Clinica Sant'Ambrogio concerned the dispute between the obstetrician and one of the nuns, who had troubles changing a male child. The obstetrician took the matter in hand and changed the baby himself before giving him to me to nurse. As I said good-bye to the Clinica, one of the nuns confided that the baby had been christened very quietly, just in case, which relieved me to no end.

When I brought back my baby to Cerro, I enjoyed most the very early mornings, when I nursed him on the balcony overlooking the lake, watching the mists dispelled by the first rays of the sun that turned the snows of Monte Rosa and the Alps golden-pink. One of my great problems was that the infant had to be weighed before and after each feeding, to see if he had absorbed the right amount of ounces of mother's milk. The infant hated to be weighed, he screamed and kicked, and I can still see myself holding him on the baby scale while Anthony tried to read it properly. The doctor's orders were not easy to follow.

In spite of the happiness brought by a healthy baby, the spell of the summer was broken. War was in the air, just before the Munich Accords between Hitler and Chamberlain. Anthony, now totally restored, left for England, just in case he should be called up. That summer, we had one large party, to which my father invited all the people to whom he owed an invitation. For the occasion, the fanciest *pâtissier* in Milan baked an enormous cake with pink frosting, which was one meter (forty inches) in diameter and about ten inches tall. In order to bring this cake out to Cerro, my father had to hire a car, since it would not have been possible to take the monster on the usual train.

One Sunday morning in late August, my father came to Cerro from Milan. He was very agitated and said, without wasting time, that I was to leave Italy immediately: in the case of war, which seemed imminent, I would be interned as a British citizen.

He would take me to the Italian-Swiss frontier, about two hours drive from us, in a friend's car. I wasted no time, bundling up my baby and putting on the only real dress I had in Cerro besides my old cotton shifts. It was a wraparound blue maternity number and old-fashioned even then, besides being miles too big for me by this time. (I had planned to buy a stunning new wardrobe later in Milan, just before going back to England in the late fall.) The trouble was that we had no money in the house; in a hurry my mother borrowed what she could from the caretaker, and we drove off to Domodossola, on the Italian-Swiss border. Here my father, pulling rank as a German consul, managed first to persuade the Italian passport authorities to let me leave the country without the necessary exit visa and, then, the Swiss passport authorities to let me into their country without the proper visa. What persuaded them to go against the strict passport regulation of the time was, he told me later, was that I was going straight through to Paris on the next international express, which was due within minutes. The train came even before my father had finished talking and he put me on it, and off I went.

At the Swiss-French border, I had to persuade the Swiss authorities to let me leave their country and the French to let me travel into theirs. It speaks for the troubles of the period that I was allowed to go from one country to another without any papers and not enough money to buy milk for the baby. However, he did not suffer from starvation, since I had the foresight to grab one of the bottles filled with sugared boiled water from which he drank whenever he did not want any more mother's milk. As for myself, I only hoped that in Paris I would have enough money to get a taxi to take me to the flat of an English journalist friend, and prayed that he would be at home and not roaming about in Europe reporting on the supercharged atmosphere of the Continent. I must have been a pitiful, but respectable, figure of a disheveled woman with a baby when I arrived in Paris, so much so that the taxi driver would not accept the few Italian *lire* that I offered him. Mercifully, my friend was at home. After feeding me, and after I fed the baby, he urged me to go immediately to Cook's Travel Agency to get a ticket to England. This I did, with the baby, to find myself engulfed by a sea of worried English people, all of whom wanted to go back home, and wailed their wishes loudly to the distressed travel agency personnel. Being tossed about, I knew that I had no chance of getting waited on. Thus I followed my friend's advice; he had foreseen the situation. I pinched the baby in my arms so hard that he yelled and shrieked so loudly as to bring on the throng's hushed silence. I kept on pinching the yelling infant until I got my ticket to London for the next day; this happened in record time.

Several months later, Anthony, the baby, and I left Billingham and England for America forever. I was happy beyond belief, because I knew that at last I could live for good in the one country in the world that spelled home to me. Now I could truthfully say:

"Heureux qui comme Ulysse, a fait un beau voyage."